Pour

THE SECRET EFFECTS OF GIVING
AND SERVING IN BUSINESS & LEADERSHIP

Published by:
Mitchell Productions, LLC
www.Mitchell-Productions.com

Editing
Stacy Hawkins Adams
www.StacyHawkinsAdams.com

Cover and Interior Design
DHBonner Virtual Solutions, LLC
www.dhbonner.net

ISBN for print version: 978-1-7333754-1-2

Wendy Lee   Maria Davis-Pierre   Andrea Davis   Carmen Jimenez-Pride
Kimberly Lawson   Cynthia Campbell   Edwinette Moses   Eulica Kimber
Lisa Williams   Toni Winston   Stacy Hawkins Adams

Pour

THE SECRET EFFECTS OF GIVING
AND SERVING IN BUSINESS & LEADERSHIP

Compiled By
Sharvette Mitchell

To my dad, Willie Howard Mitchell (RIP)

Who gave me my first job of raking the leaves, who taught me how to play tennis and supported me at my matches in middle school, who taught me how to drive because my sister (Kym) and I shot my mom's nerves to pieces and who always bought us a candy bar EVERY time we went to the store until one day, he stopped... He turned to me and said, "You are not going to get everything you want in life". I was mad that day but now I understand. #POUR

Contents

Foreword

Hey girl hey, and hey guys, too! I'm Toni M. Winston and I'm excited to share with you this awesome book written by Sharvette Mitchell and her group of clients. I have had the privilege of knowing Sharvette for many years — initially as an acquaintance whose vision, implementation and results I greatly respected. However, in the past five years, we have moved from granting mutual respect from afar to forging a friendship for which I'm grateful. We have shared many laughs and giggles, worked on various projects and watched things and people take shape and excel.

When I heard that Sharvette was working on a new book and the title would be POUR, I thought, "How fitting!" Pouring is what I see her do daily in her personal life, on her social media accounts and with her clients. What you should know is that having the ability to pour doesn't always come easy. Many people, whether in business or in their personal lives, believe that the time to pour into others is when they can say "My cup runneth over." During a season of overflow, it seems quite natural to want to give and share what you have because you are in a position of surplus. But what about when the glass seems half full?

Half full, you say? Yes, half full. When our glasses are half full, we often think we don't have enough to share or that we need others to pour into us and fill us up, so that we'll have some to share. Well, I'm a "church girl" through and through, and considering what it means to be half full made me think back to my Sunday School lessons on the biblical passage in 2 Kings, in which the prophet Elijah asked a widow what she had to offer and she told him that all she possessed was a jar of oil. According to the Toni M. Winston (TMW) paraphrase of this parable, Elijah asked her to go far and near to collect vessels to fill, and to not just get a few, but to get many. He asked her to take them home and to pour that one jar of oil into each of the vessels she had collected, until they were full. As the story goes (in both versions), once she declared "There is not another vessel" to fill, the oil stopped flowing. At this point, Elijah advised the widow to go and sell the oil and pay her debts and live off of the rest.

The moral of this story and its relation to my "half full" analogy? This woman did not wait until she believed that she had enough for herself and her family to move forward, and neither should you! Although you may view your cup as half full, this doesn't mean that what you have to offer in your business or your life isn't ready to share. Sharvette and the writers featured in this book provide great examples of the ability to pour, not from only what they have as established business women and entrepreneurs, but also as they learn new skills, create new training and develop new content. They are continuously pouring.

I'm so glad that you have decided to grab a copy of this book. I believe the anecdotes, stories and principles shared in POUR will change your life, and the lives of those around you. As you read these chapters, be encouraged to pour wherever you are in your journey. Don't wait until you think you have exactly what you need. Your ability to pour will create the abundance that you desire, and Sharvette and her clients are here to show you the way.

I can't wait to drink from your cup! Enjoy the read.

~ Toni M. Winston
Follow The Pink Squirrel

Introduction

At the time this book was being compiled, our world was experiencing a global health pandemic — COVID-19. The participating authors had to write their chapters while in quarantine, with some homeschooling children and fighting to find paper towels along with operating businesses and/or working full-time jobs. Amid tremendous uncertainty, deep loss and grief, and widespread anxiety, they somehow managed to produce.

How do you write during a crisis? What do you put on paper during a pandemic? Here's the answer: You POUR.

Our friends on Dictonary.com define POUR as:
pour | /pôr/ | verb

- flow rapidly in a steady stream
- prepare and serve
- express one's feelings or thoughts in a full and unrestrained way

The epitome of these definitions is what you will find weaved into the upcoming chapters, penned by entrepreneurs and leaders from around the nation.

I selected the title for this book, in part, because of a sermon that my pastor, Bishop Joel V. Brown, preached. The word POUR was in a scripture he referenced one Sunday, and it leapt out at me and resonated every time he uttered it.

> *"...and see if I won't throw open the windows of heaven*
> *for you and POUR out on you blessing without measure."*
> *Malachi 3:10 (ISV)*

So listen: I don't know if you are reading this book the year it was released or 20 years later. What I can affirm for you, without any doubt in my mind, is that your posture of serving and pouring will always pay off — in both your personal life and for your business, organization or brand. For, one naturally flows into the other, with your personal preparation and serving often beginning long before your business is established and successful.

I encourage you to consciously consume all that the authors share, so that your own pouring can flow from greater intention and yield greater impact.

#POUR

~ Sharvette Mitchell
Visionary Author, Online Strategist and Internet Talk Radio Host

Whole Vessels Hold More Water

By Wendy Lee

The biggest irony is that this once shy, timid, scared, paranoid, super-sensitive, intimidated, easily embarrassed little girl, then teenager, eventually young adult and now grown woman stands before crowds slinging jokes and sharing her story.

Growing up in an era where children had no voice, opinion or say in the affairs of their own lives, I wasn't asked how I felt or what I thought. This routinely left me feeling like my opinion didn't matter, and as result, I didn't fully develop my voice and my sense of self.

At age 17, however, the spiritual leaders in my life helped me identify my gifts and began to nurture them. I learned that I could sing, dance, help others and even draw. Finally, I felt useful, necessary, valuable and wanted.

Seven years later, while attending a church-based talent show on a whim, I chuckled to myself when the emcee asked for more participants. After the third plea, however, I decided to help. For the first time ever, I volunteered to stand before an audience of strangers and tell a few jokes. While I figured this would be a kind and caring audience of Christians, I had all the hallmarks of stage fright: sweaty palms, tickling fingers, butterflies in the stomach, racing heart, dry throat and shaky knees. Somehow, though, I held myself together long enough to repeat several goofy jokes that I recalled from child-hood; and to my surprise they were well received.

As I returned to my pew, the pastor of the church called me to the pulpit. He prayed for me and declared to me and to the watching congregation that I would travel to share more humor and that God would place me before great men. The pastor then led the congregation in collecting an offering for me, as seed for the future harvest.

Little did I know that on that night 14 years ago, he was prophe-sying my destiny. This was the beginning of my journey into freedom and into the unveiling of Wendy Lee, a woman walking in purpose, rather than just the "Quietstorm" comedienne having fun that I had viewed myself to be.

I must be honest and share that the transformation did not happen overnight. Even as churches began inviting me to perform, I had zero direction, zero mission and minimal ambition. When I performed my comedy routines I was "just having fun," with little intention or strategy for growing a business or reaching more people through the ministry of humor. I tremendously enjoyed making others laugh. For seven years I did this, oblivious to the fact that I had a source of income in my possession.

In fact, I didn't summon the motivation to pursue something more with this gift until seven years after that pastor's declaration, when I attended a conference for Christian comedians. That journey from Petersburg, Virginia to Nashville, Tennessee remains memo-rable not only for the insight it gave me into the power of comedy, but also for being the first place I met and connected with my "tribe"– about 25 men and women who loved God and appreciated

2

humor as much as I did.

Prior to meeting them, I felt strange and alone. (Honestly, I often still feel that way, but I embrace it now and use it as fuel). This conference served as my catalyst for acknowledging that I was a comedian, led me to adopt a stage name and helped me transform my hobby of performing comedy into a business. Motivated by spending three days with veteran spirit-filled comedians, I came home and created flyers and business cards to send to local churches, requesting an opportunity to exercise my gift.

From that point on, I have been performing on a routine basis — monthly for certain, and oftentimes weekly. The vision that pastor spoke over me came to fruition: I have traveled the United States and have been in the presence of well-known and well-respected people. I have now turned my focus toward seizing international opportunities before influential audiences of all kinds.

During my development, insightful strangers have seen more than a comedian. They also have seen my gifts of strength, influence, leadership and the ability to transform the atmosphere of a room. I slowly began to realize that bringing my humor was about more than just bringing the fun and having a good time doing it.

As I grew into awareness of my potential, several female ministers poured into me with their time, mentorship, patience, love and leadership. Each of these women helped me discover my voice, and it was an epiphany. *"Oh my God!* I have something to say! What?! Something other than jokes? You want to know my view on this? My opinion counts? You're really listening to me?"

Not only that, but on rare occasions, when the stars and moon properly aligned, wisdom, knowledge and profound teaching would pour out of me. Had those awesome ladies not afforded me their support and a constant space to express myself, I'd be stuck thinking that belly laughs were all I was good for. Yet, as a result of being poured into, I was able to see value and use in myself, and that took me to the next phase of my journey.

Interestingly and in divine time, these ladies showed up after a season when there was a battle raging within me — against Wendy Lee and Comedian Quietstorm. These two had a serious dislike for one another. Quietstorm wanted the stage all of the time. That chick didn't know how to sit herself down unless there was another comedian in the room. Wendy Lee resented Quietstorm for coming along and stealing her light — overtaking, standing in front of and blotting out the depth of who she was.

Folks! What turmoil to be at odds with oneself! Could these two get along and coexist? Or would one of them have to die? This was the constant battle raging within me, for several years; and not only within, but also from without — including people telling me I couldn't be a comedian and a minister. "You cannot teach biblical principals in a comedic way. Who's going to take you seriously?" they would say. Clearly these people had never heard of renowned ministers Joyce Meyers and Jesse Duplantis — or Wendy Lee.

Allow me to backtrack. In 2001, I was licensed as a lay minister by my local church assembly. However, it wasn't until 11 years later that I preached my first message, as a guest minister for a local church, when I received the invitation out of the blue. The following year, I was asked by a pastor in Texas to partner as a podcast teacher for that congregation's online church. For 18 months, I would share practical and spiritual messages each week on various topics.

Still y'all! I did not feel myself coming into my own. From 2013 to this day, in the year 2020, I have continued my journey to self-discovery. Oh the hard, painful lessons, the aha moments, the frustration, the constantly wanting to quit, but knowing I've come too far to stop or turn back, the constantly asking myself, "Why the heck is this happening?"

There also have been thoughts of "I cannot take any more of this!" and the questioning of "God where are you?" My answers came in realizing that my being alive was proof that God was still present with me.

People! Folks! Dear readers of mine! Can I tell you that 2014 through 2019 were five years of hell in my personal earth? The flames of hell's internal fire ravaged my soul for 1,140 days/27,360 hours. It is said one must do a thing for 10,000 hours to be considered an expert. Ladies and gentleman, that be me! I am an expert in being a long-term resident and successfully moving out of a personal hell! Thank you for your applause.

During my residency, I mastered the art of hiding in plain sight; being physically present but mentally/emotionally absent; retreating into the background; blending in; playing small; watching numerous opportunities pass me by, and purposely dulling my shine because I did not want to be seen or remembered. Yes, I was intentionally attempting to sabotage my life as well as my comedy career, because I was tired of living, but afraid to die. I didn't want to breathe because it took too much energy. I needed a break. I wanted to press "pause" on the universe so I could get myself together. I was already shattered — just waiting for my proverbial glass to break.

Do not be sad for me. This pathway through hell would eventually lead to personal freedom. For me, it was literally a dark-est-hour-before-dawn experience. It was also the longest five-year hour ever!!! Somebody's clock stopped working and her calendar didn't flip.

This darkness caused me to see myself. I know that sounds back-wards, but this was my experience. I saw that I was broken; I saw that I needed professional help; I saw that life wasn't going to go well for me unless I addressed some of my issues.

What issues? Number one, for years I thought that I had no voice. Consequently, I allowed people to do whatever and say whatever to me without doing anything about it. I went along just to get along. I was overly agreeable because I was uncomfortable with conflict and confrontation. As a result, I was undercover resentful for all of the negative things that ever happened to me (many I allowed because I was afraid to exercise and enforce my right to say "no"). I did not know my power. I presented myself like a stray cat, when in actuality I was a lioness.

Secondly, I was hiding, y'all. Showing up with just enough per-sonality to perform onstage, while otherwise being enveloped in darkness and solitude. The darkness and solitude of this "cave" were familiar, comfortable and safe. Deception and fear told me that the cave was freedom, as it would mentally take me anywhere that I desired to go. I hated myself because I was not being the authentic Wendy Lee. Sadly, I didn't even know who that authen-tic Wendy Lee was, because I tried so hard to fit the mold of who I thought others wanted me to be. By spending years attempting to fit a nonexistent mold, I totally lost, or more accurately, I never

WHOLE VESSELS HOLD MORE WATER

even tapped into, the true person of Wendy Lee.

Literally, this darkness I refer to as hell was where I was discovering myself. Prior to this, all I knew about myself was that I love the color red and everything that had sugar in it. Some people have a sweet tooth, but the full set of my choppers are sweet! So here I was, entering middle age with no clue about who I was. To add pressure, I was frustrated about not knowing my identity and fed up with the imposter who was now loved by many AND adding nice supplementary income to my household.

I finally accepted that I had to deal with the ugly truth — the love/hate relationship I had with myself. Due to being a fearful, passive pushover, I bucked and rebelled at everything I didn't like, because that made me feel empowered and unafraid. My soft persona and even-keeled temperament could quickly transform into rage when I felt threatened or challenged. Anyone looking from the outside would label this as bipolar. That is not so! I only like warm weather, so I know that I'm unipolar. Lol!

Actually, I did seek help from a professional — several to be exact. Allow me to insert that this decision did not come easy; it took several months of miserable days to give in to this necessity. Being super Christian, I was of the mindset that Jesus and prayer alone were the answer to everything. Talks with broader-minded Christians allowed me to expand my belief system and add therapy to my toolbox of solutions. Part of my belief system had been that therapy was for crazy people. Yet, here's a secret I didn't tell anyone: During my time in hell, I felt crazy more often than not. I felt so out of control, so conflicted, so empty, so hollow inside. My mind felt like a ball of yarn, my soul ached, as did my heart.

I walked around disappointed because no one could hear the silent cry of my heart. That cry was, "Help me! I don't want to be like this!" The only phrases being said to me were, "Tell me a joke or "Make me laugh" or "When are you performing again?" or "Remember me when you get big."

When I was honest to that usually insincere, habitual question, "How are you?" my answer of, "Not very well" was taken as a joke. That was partially my doing, as I'd learned to laugh off, mask, disregard, downplay and minimize my own feelings. Why should anyone care or pay attention when I ignored and belittled them for so long? By example, I was showing people to treat me as I treated myself.

In case you're wondering what the psychotherapists said. . . there were no chemical imbalances. I needed talk therapy to unpack my compressed emotions. That is, emotions that never got expressed because I had been sweeping them under the proverbial rug. After doing that for so long, those emotions ran out of space and started to spill over into every area of my life.

Listen! Your spirit and your body know when things are out of balance and will let you know so. Listen to your body. Pay attention to your spirit. My intuition knew many things were out of sync, although there were church folks telling me that nothing was wrong, and to pray more and speak positively. Thank God for counsel, but our inner guidance system NEVER steers us wrong. My inner spirit led me to get professional help for my mind and emotions, so they could reach a healthier state.

Now, let me tell the entire truth, because I know that last paragraph sounded like the fairytale ending of a Disney movie. Well! That's not my testimony. I went through about ten different therapists before finding one where we both felt a good match. Prior to number ten, there were two which I wanted to keep, but THEY fired ME. You'll have to book me to find out the details.

As I weave the business side of all this background into this story of my journey, let me say this. . . You must be the biggest advocate for yourself in all that you do. No one should fight harder for your health and wholeness than you. No one should invest more into your ministry, your craft or your business than you.

Let me explain a little deeper. As with most things, the majority of work is done behind the scenes. My spiritual growth, for example, was and is up to me, with the majority of the work being done outside of church services and other worship gatherings. In business, time spent in the office, at my store or on the stage or platform is part of my preparation. Selling products and services, performing, speaking, producing, leading, hosting and such cannot be effective if the behind-the-scenes work is not regularly done. So in regard to therapy, I studied, researched, read, listened to broadcasts, etc. – seeking out anything in relation to mental health and healing and wholeness that I could, outside of my counseling sessions. My healing was ultimately up to me.

How did all of my issues affect my business? Possessing an underdeveloped voice affected my confidence, self-esteem and self-image. In order to really be successful and thrive, we must know who we are and what we have to offer. Whoever and whatever we are in our private lives is mirrored in every arena (family, friendships, workplace, business) of our lives. It behooves us to be diligent about becoming whole, balanced individuals before constantly putting ourselves in the presence of people in a leadership capacity.

My comedy routines reflected my lack of confidence, low self-esteem and poor self-image. I was showing up to engagements looking any type of way. I was not as captivating as my audiences likely expected, because my confidence was zero. I relied on the audience response instead of owning the stage and *creating* the audience response.

Today, Wendy Lee/Quietstorm walks to the mic knowing that she belongs there. She is funny and she's here to make you laugh, think and rethink! You will pee in your pants. We as business owners MUST walk into whatever room or platform knowing that we belong there and that we're going to engage those we are there to serve.

Out of fear, I had avoided performing at certain venues or entering certain competitions for the longest. I chose not to hang out with other comics because I didn't feel like I was good enough or worthy enough to be a part of their circle. My self-talk was horrible as well as my thought life.

As part of my transformation, I created a daily routine of positive self-talk and positive thinking. I had to be intentional about loving and valuing myself. I was responsible for ALL of my healing and the implementation of it.

What are you telling yourself? Whatever we think about ourselves shows up in our presentation. The outside is a reflection of what's happening inside.

When I felt better about myself as an individual, my business practices improved and my income increased, because confidence is attractive. Confidence draws certain people to you. I began to pursue engagements, enter competitions and market myself. I was no longer afraid of rejection, because I changed my perspective on it — rejection is either protection or a "not now, try again later" signal.

Speaking of fear, what a life stealer! Nothing is wrong with feeling fearful. The problem occurs when we allow it to paralyze us or become our decision maker. Daily I encounter things that cause me to fear. That feeling may never completely leave me, but it will no longer cause me to miss out on opportunities. Numerous things I was most fearful of yielded me my greatest results in the form of connections, more bookings, more sales and greater opportunities.

Here's my final thought: Because God has sent numerous people throughout my journey to pour various blessings and pieces of wisdom into me, I can in turn pour into others. Life is reciprocal like that. Whatever we pour into others will eventually get poured into the next. It behooves us to make sure we are pouring from a clean vessel with no leaks. Most importantly, make sure you are pouring into yourself, as *you* are your greatest asset.

How Impact Multiplies
When Used For Good

By Maria Davis-Pierre, LMHC

"Success is to be measured not so much by the position that one has reached in life as by the obstacles which he has overcome while trying to succeed."
– Booker T. Washington

I'm a licensed therapist by trade. I like to help people; it has always been my calling. Prior to having my first child, I truly had no aspirations to build a brand or a platform. All I knew was that I wanted my own private practice so I could be my own boss.

As soon as I obtained my Florida state license in 2014, I opened my private practice. Around that same time, my husband and I learned that our daughter, who was then 18 months old, was autistic.

Anyone who has been through a process like this knows it's not easy. I advocated for months to get a diagnosis for what I had suspected for a while to be the answer to questions about her development. Once my husband and I received official word that it was indeed autism, I threw myself full force into figuring out what we should be doing to set our daughter up for success.

I learned everything about the school system and its special education programming, and about the laws associated with special education. You name it, I researched it. This was necessary, because unfortunately, we had no one to walk us through this process. I was just handed the paperwork that confirmed her condition and left to my own devices.

All the while, I still had my private therapy practice and wanted it to thrive, and I was doing my best to keep the business afloat amid my parenting demands. To be honest, my efforts were lackluster. The passion I might have poured into the practice was mostly redirected to my passion for giving my daughter the best chance at an independent life. That had become my primary focus, leaving the business in secondary position.

As I got more acquainted with how to advocate for my daughter, some of the friends and acquaintances in our social circle, and the parents of students at my daughter's school, noticed how involved I was. They not only recognized that I was not ashamed of my child and that I did the best I could to speak up for her needs — but also how successful I was at doing so.

They began to ask me for help. They wanted to know the secret to how I, as a black mother, felt comfortable being so open about my daughter and her autism diagnosis. How could I so easily share my story and have no fears nor cares about the black community "labeling" my daughter, they asked?

Truth is, in that moment when my daughter was diagnosed, I wasn't shocked, I wasn't numb, I wasn't ashamed. I wasn't even sad. I didn't really feel any of those emotions that a lot of parents say they experience when their child is diagnosed.

My sole focus was on my child and how the world would treat her — and label her. I don't mean a label in terms of stigmas related to mental health or disabilities. For me, it meant that here she was, a black autistic girl. It's hard enough being black. Add girl in and that is another layer. Now we were having to include autism, and I instinctively knew that would be another layer of ignorance she would face. This is what truly fueled me to become the advocate that I am for her.

My husband saw the results I was achieving for our daughter and also how my helping other black parents learn to advocate for their children was making a difference. After a few months, he began encouraging me to merge what had become my two top priorities outside of caring for our family — autism advocacy and my therapy business. In one conversation I jokingly entertained him: "Yeah," I said, "I should start *Autism in Black*."

He was serious, though. "That's genius!" was his immediate response.

Initially, I downplayed the possibility. But after giving it some thought, I had to admit it was a solid business idea — one I wasn't necessarily ready to execute. I couldn't pinpoint why — I already was advocating, and the resources I had uncovered in researching programs and services for my daughter had been helpful to many of the parents to whom I had offered my guidance and advice. They would not have been as informed otherwise.

What finally made me take the idea seriously was acknowledging what I knew from experience: Many available resources really don't make their way into our community. If we don't know about them, we can't access them. Additionally, the black community is often misinformed about what autism is and the fact that it should be treated as a condition, not as a life sentence. We have so many stigmas to deal with, not only outside of our community, but also within our community. I mean, here I was, an actual healthcare provider, and I had to fire many of my daughter's therapists because of their lack of cultural responsiveness and parental support.

My husband pushed me to believe in myself and make Autism in Black® more than just a casual conversation topic. Yet, I was so scared to venture out and start this new business. Constantly feeling the imposter syndrome (even to this day), I hemmed and hawed and procrastinated. But he was right, because unknowingly, I had put myself in an expert position. I had taken countless trainings and conducted hours upon hours of research.

I finally got so tired of hearing him talk about it that I obtained a business license for the brand (Autism in Black®) to keep the peace! However, by this time we had added a boy and girl — twins — to the crew. So again, I had to focus on something other than business. I needed to help our oldest adjust to being a big sister, and I had to adjust to being a mom to three kids. (It's a delicate balance to this day. I often feel like I'm juggling glass balls and can't afford to drop any of them.)

As a result, I have to admit that for a while in the beginning, I was just toying with the idea of Autism in Black; doing stuff here and there, and turning down a lot of opportunities. I wasn't even really doing therapy in my private practice anymore. My days revolved around keeping track of the progress our eldest was making and the goals she was achieving, while ensuring that our twins also felt cared for and loved.

In 2018, my husband had a long talk with me about my gift and the platform that I could be building. He also let me know that I shouldn't feel pressured to do it alone. I needed to ask for help and be okay with it.

He has always been my voice of reason, and his vision for me has always been so much greater than my vision for myself. I had to quit fighting it and accept my gift. But I was scared, so scared. Was there such a thing as work-life balance? How could I run a successful business and still be the advocate I had become for my daughter? Where was I going to find the time to be a mom, wife, entrepreneur and all of the other roles I played?

Again, this is where my husband came in, with a loving, but *not* gentle push — more like a swift kick — off the cliff. He insisted that I stop thinking of the reasons I couldn't do it and instead consider all of the families that would suffer if they didn't have access to my expertise.

That's when it clicked for me. My perspective shifted. I asked and answered my own pivotal questions: *Who is out here advocating for black families? Who is giving us the right information?* Because let's face it, the reality is that there is a gap between white children getting diagnosed and black children getting diagnosed. A primary reason is the misinformation that our community has about autism. It is seen as the big bad boogie monster.

I realized that I had a responsibility to get the right information to our community, and at the same time, an opportunity to break some of those generational curses within our community. You know the ones I am talking about: Ignoring something and just hoping it will go away, or just praying about something with no action, or keeping secrets or thinking that physical punishment can "cure" anything.

As I pondered all of this, I relied on a favorite quote by President Barak Obama – one that I still refer to when I need a good push: "Change will not come if we wait for some other person or some other time. We are the ones we've been waiting for. We are the change that we seek."

He was right. I couldn't just sit and notice these disparities and not take action. So I set my intention to move, to stop playing from the sidelines with my business and get in the game.

I am a person who is able to sit down with other black families and help them understand that we can stay true to our faith and still seek professional help. It has been gratifying to see the strides the children and families I work with have made, as a result of my care and coaching. Watching other parents learn how to advocate and secure resources for their autistic children has been just as rewarding as experiencing the success of advocating for my daughter.

I would be lying if I said just jumping into the game was easy. This journey has been difficult, extremely difficult. As the parent of a child with a disability, I have often felt like I couldn't or shouldn't be focusing on my own goals or ambitions. That mom guilt is real!

Many of us in this situation focus so much on the day to day of what it takes to raise a child with a disability that we constantly put ourselves last. It is common, and yes, even I, the therapist struggled with this.

However, why do we think that we can't have it all? Why is it that when we have children, we get so wrapped up in making sure they turn out to be decent human beings that we lose ourselves?

These are questions that I asked myself. Why was I so afraid of succeeding and building a well-known brand?

I know we have all heard the quote "Feel the fear and do it anyway." Ah, yeah...that doesn't always work. You can feel that fear and stop dead in your tracks. That fear can cause some real deep anxiety, and as a result, you can get caught up in a stressful cycle of trying to avoid what is causing it. Before you know it, time has passed, and you feel as if you can't make up for it, so you become even more discouraged.

Well you can't make up for lost time, but you can start somewhere. A small step is progress compared to doing nothing. I want to give you the truth: That fear may never go away, but you can get comfortable with the uneasy feelings it brings along and move forward anyway. It took me a while to figure out and own that the fear holding me back boiled down to mom guilt.

I had to get out of the mindset that doing something that I enjoyed and that was for me made me a bad mom. Instead, I had to own that it made me a better one. I also realized that having genuine people rooting for me was crucial to my success. Having such a supportive husband who pushed — and continues to push me — outside of my comfort zone was a blessing.

Every time I support a client and hear that person say how having my services has made it so much easier for his or her family, I gain more drive to keep pushing. Everything that has been poured into me I pour right back into them.

I have days where I kill it professionally. I'm talking about taking meetings, speaking and supporting my clients. And then there are days where I don't get one thing accomplished because I had to kill it as a mom. What I've learned is that it's okay to give myself grace, because I'm still making an impact.

That's what I want for you, too. We come up with so many reasons in our mind about why we can't step out and start our business or take it to the next level — lack of money, time, resources, etc., Trust me — I know that some of these reasons are valid. However, I encourage you to start somewhere.

Start with one small step, because even a single step is progress. Take the time to figure out what you want to do and don't feel pressured by those around you. Embrace your gifts and don't hide them. Be confident in them. Acknowledge the truths in this additional quote that I love: "You may not control all the events that happen to you, but you can decide not to be reduced by them." – Maya Angelou

I had no control over having a child with a disability and the impact that it would have on me as a parent. It's a job, and those of you in similar situations understand. However, rather than be reduced by it, we can take our experiences and use them to help others — not just by being an advocate, but in so many other ways, too. What I have gained most from nurturing and advocating for my daughter is patience, and we all know that patience can be used in so many ways. So, take whatever nuggets you have from your experiences and use them to pour into others.

I couldn't end this chapter without giving you some good entrepreneurial and therapeutic advice:

1. Rely on your support circle. It's okay; asking for help doesn't make you any less of a parent or person. I learned that asking

for help was a sign that I was practicing good self-care, and that weakness is *not* asking for help and suffering in silence.

2. Boundaries are your best friend. Cut toxic people out of your inner circle. I learned to set boundaries based on my core values and what was realistic for me to remain healthy and positive, instead of giving preference to other people's values, wants and needs.

3. Don't let fear or shame stand in the way. Or at least don't let it stand in your way for too long. Push through it, little by little.

4. Give yourself grace. Balance is a hard thing to accomplish; and honestly, I don't know if it's truly possible, as balance means something different for everyone. So give yourself grace to make mistakes and figure out what works for you.

5. We are never going to find the right time to start something, because we will always find a reason we can't. The time is now.

I Was Born For This

By Andrea Davis

As I drove out of the gate of Goddard Space Flight Center on my final day of a 35-year career as a federal employee, the cocktail of emotions coursing through me was overwhelming. I felt a sense of relief and joy; but there also was some fear and uncertainty, mixed with sadness, and topped off with a splash of loss and grief.

I was full of joy that I had completed a journey I began at the age of twenty-three, and relieved that the painful and disappointing experiences that had played a significant role in shaping and molding me, were now only punctuations in the story of my life. Yet, the uncertainty of how my second half would turn out laced these positive feelings with fear. In brief moments, sadness two-stepped with grief, at thoughts of leaving all that was familiar, and all that I knew, to embark upon a new journey and enter a new chapter. This was an intoxicating combination.

Later, as I reflected on that day and on my entire career as a federal employee, I also found myself filled with gratitude. My government career had carried me to the place I find myself today. It provided a means to the resources I needed to raise my son as a single parent. At times, I even let it define me and determine my value — until I met my purpose. Ultimately, my work helped prepare me for the roles of life coach, author, speaker and entrepreneur that I now embrace.

The first half of my life carried me to the business I am building, the passions I am pursuing, and the vision I've developed for the second half of my life. It strengthened my resolve to do more, be more and have more, beyond my job title or responsibilities or the challenges that came with that work. The biblical scripture Job 8:7 exemplifies what I mean: "Though thy beginning was small, yet thy latter end should greatly increase."

At first glance, however, the two worlds may seem to have nothing in common. How could a career as a federal contracting officer catapult me into serving as a life coach, author, speaker and business owner? Before I retired, I took every opportunity that presented itself to pour into others, especially women in a state of pain or hopeless, or those who needed to know they had options and the power to change or overcome any situation they encountered. I was energized after every encounter. There were times when my desire to pour into others caused me to have to make up time after hours, sometimes until 9 p.m. or 10 p.m., to meet milestones in my project schedules. But it was worth it. Deep down inside, I felt my worth increase and my confidence rise each time I offered someone my support.

I started to see that I was born to pour into the lives of women, especially those struggling to move into a place of significance and abundance in the second half of life — women like me. I was already serving in a ministry for survivors of sexual abuse. And while I wanted to provide therapy, since I was untrained in that field, I could instead help them see that even out of their most deplorable pain, a life of significance and power could be born. After all, if it could be done in renowned minister Joyce Meyer's life (one example), it surely could be done in theirs.

I realized I was born to show women what it looks like to overcome disappointment, heartache and roadblocks; to finally get routed to the road of purpose and destiny. My career in federal government, for example, was meant to be temporary, but became a lifeline when I separated from my husband a year into my first job with the government. The benefits, opportunity to travel, and early successes were like golden handcuffs. And after the birth of my son, it simply seemed impossible to leave and not be deemed unreasonable by those around me who would question whether I was being responsible.

Later, I just felt stuck and couldn't see that I had any other options. Before I knew it, I was twenty, then twenty-five, then thirty years in, and it made no sense to just up and leave, even though I was frustrated, and eventually felt insignificant. I realized later that my career was what in the military is known as a proving ground — an area where weapons or other military technology are experimented with or tested. In the same vein, I had to be proven, tried and tested in order to be launched into my destiny with all that I carry now.

In that process, I picked up some keen negotiating, critical thinking and problem mitigation skills that have served me well as an entrepreneur. But more importantly, I learned to tap into my passion, and see the value of my gifts and talents to build a life I now love — one that brings significance to my life and to those I serve. The things that stir my emotions, that tug at my heart strings, were brought to light during my career; and the "come up" from where I was and what I endured to where I am now and where I'm headed is nothing short of divine. While my two worlds seemed to be totally opposite, they met at the crossroads of destiny and purpose.

Coming to a place of understanding who I am, including my talents and gifts, took place during those 35 years as a government employee. I had some great highs during my career, especially during the early years. The awards, promotions, accolades and recognition came fast and furious. Unfortunately, the last few years before retirement were quite the opposite.

I'm not sure exactly when the downturn started, but it led from one disappointment to another, with me receiving one hollow explanation after another from management after being passed over for promotions, time after time. Eventually, I began to feel like a size 10 foot trying to fit into a size 8 shoe — feeling squeezed, uncomfortable and frustrated.

As grateful as I was to have had opportunities to work in various positions at the agencies I served, those roles never fit that well, even in the earlier years. Now, on the day I left work for the last time, I could put all of that behind me. I realized this as the emotions that had swirled inside me on that final drive home began to settle. I was on my way to building a bigger life. A life that would allow me to be unapologetically who I was meant to be.

I could breathe differently, knowing that I could now focus on doing what fed my soul and helped others, such as the times I spent counseling a co-worker how to maintain her faith while going through a separation or coaching a young man I met in training how to change career fields to better his life, or helping a mentee articulate her strengths and her value to prepare for a job interview.

If I'd understood then what I began to understand during my iPEC Coach Training, I could have looked at things from a different perspective sooner, and come to the understanding that where I was and what I was enduring was actually the proving ground for where I was going and what I was to become. I believe the journey to my new life as an entrepreneur and ministry leader, life coach, author and speaker would have been easier, despite the valleys. I wonder, though, if my passion to see women come into the knowledge of the power they possess and the possibilities available to them when they align it with their purpose would be as deep as it is. I believe that everything builds from each experience and season, and each building block is important.

One person I credit with pouring into me through her work is speaker, life coach and author Lisa Nichols. In 2015, I listened to her audiobook *Abundance Now*, and its messages started me on the path to believing that I could have a life where I could be more, do more and have more. I didn't have a vision for what that bigger, more abundant life looked like, or even how to go after it, but Ms. Nichol's book inspired me to dream for a bigger, bolder more purposeful life.

I took two important challenges from that book. The first was to be brave enough to open my mouth and say what I want. Oftentimes we don't say out loud what we want. We miss the opportunity to put our dreams in the atmosphere, for fear that we will be talked about or viewed as too old, too ill-equipped, too uneducated, too short, too tall, too broke, too late, too much of an introvert. We are afraid of what others will say because of our previous public failures witnessed by them. And there are those private failures that we hold onto that keep us from moving forward as we play the narratives of those life lessons over and over in our minds.

The other detail that resonated with me while reading *Abundance Now* was Lisa's account of sending a check to the bank every time she got paid, writing her goal in the memo each time: "investing in my future." That left a big impression on me. It spoke of the power of believing in what you want and investing even the smallest amount consistently.

Four years before I actually left the government, I started trying to figure out what I could or would do upon my departure. What kind of work could I do to serve those I was called to serve?

I was afraid that if I didn't figure something out and do it soon, I would be too old, or miss out all together and someone else would get my "slot." I hadn't yet grasped that what I was called to do was assigned to me and no one else. I didn't realize that if I would focus on discovering my purpose, and the *why* to my life, then the *what* would eventually become clear. I was stuck in fear, thinking that my gifts and talents would be taken away from me, like the man in the biblical parable who dug a hole and hid what his master had given him to work with, rather than taking it and increasing its worth.

I wasn't trying to hide my gifts and talents; I wanted to use them. So even while I fretted, I actively began pursuing a way to do what I was called to do. I began to focus on Philippians 1:6, which declares: "Being confident of this very thing, that He who has begun a good work in you will complete it until the day of Jesus Christ."

To me this meant that getting to where I was destined to go and doing what I was called to do would be a process and not a destination or a race.

After much prayer and getting some feedback from friends and co-workers about what they thought I was talented at or at least good at, I took the Basden-Johnson Spiritual Gift Analysis, which provided confirmation that coaching was my gift, and that I was already operating in it. The analysis indicated that my primary spiritual gift is exhortation, and the definition of that gift read as follows: "The ability to help others reach their full potential by means of encouraging, challenging, confronting and guiding. Essentially, it is the gift of coaching others to become all that God wants them to be." This was total confirmation for me, so I started looking into training programs. I ended up taking one that would provide what was needed to take my coaching around the world.

One of the things that stays with me even now from my nine months of iPEC training is the pre-work I was required to complete prior to the first session in March 2018. I thought it was invasive and, frankly, too much. Why did I need to be able to articulate what I wanted my life to look like in one year, three years and five years? There were even questions about: where I lived, what my house looked like, what I did in the morning, what I ate, what I did for leisure, where I vacationed, how I spent my holidays, and so on. However, all of this helped me see how important having a vison for your life is, and how living each day intentionally would get me to that life.

This is something that Bruce D. Schneider, the founder of this training program institute, would often say in our online seminars: "Trust the process." (These days, I not only remind myself to trust the process, I also encourage my clients and others to do so.) When we understand it's a process, we can be kinder to ourselves. Deep inside, I'm convinced that all of that intrusive pre-work (that was probably never read by anyone, after it was turned in) was required mostly to set the atmosphere and teach me how to articulate what is really important to me and build my life around that and set the process in motion.

Today, my life is in alignment with the very reason I was born. My values, gifts, talents, and passions are equipping me to serve at a new level. In a time when many people are seeking help to bring clarity to various areas of their life with the services of a life coach, I am ready and eager to assist. I can help them identify strengths and weaknesses to overcome obstacles holding them back.

Helping others see what they possess isn't enough. They are going to need to know how to get from where they currently are to that place where they can operate at their best. They are going to need a plan, or roadmap, and that's where a life coach comes in. I realized I had spent the last fifteen years of my federal career helping people identify the obstacles getting in the way of what they said they wanted, assisting them with finding motivation and pinpointing their resistance to change. All along in serving others I had been operating in the capacity of a life coach – honing a set of skills, talents and gifts that I could also use to start a small business.

What a difference a year makes. Knowing my purpose, and understanding how I've been equipped to carry it out, has propelled me to a new level of servant leadership. Now that I have settled into my next chapter, which is still filled with joy, excitement and quite a bit of the unknown, I no longer lace these emotions with fear or grief. I have developed a fresh perspective on life; and making small shifts in how I think about each season has brought meaning and purpose to my personal journey and to my business.

While my sphere of influence is still relatively small, every opportunity I take to serve others increases my reach, which in turn positively affects my business. While I've served in a number of leadership positions in my career and in various organizations, the positions that allowed me to use my gifts and talents unencumbered have yielded the most self-awareness, growth, opportunity and fulfilment. These are the positions that have allowed me to prepare for the successes to come in my business, as I pour into others all that they need in order to go, to lead and to thrive. I want them to know that it is never too late and they are never too old to reinvent themselves and start anew.

Falling Together

By Carmen Jimenez-Pride

My first professional position after receiving a master's degree in social work was in child protective services. As a social worker fresh out of graduate school with no major life plans and no real responsibilities, having a state job was a big accomplishment. Considering my background and family narrative, having a master's degree was more than a normal accomplishment, and being salaried with benefits was even more impressive.

During four of the eight years I spent working within the child protection system, I was content. There is a level of complacency that sets in when you're doing more than just surviving and your income is more than many of your peers.

My perspective began to change shortly after reaching my four-year mark. I wanted to advance from being a frontline worker to a supervisory position. Putting in countless applications and getting the 'Thank you for interviewing, but you did not meet the qualifications for the position' emails, as well as seeing individuals who had not been with the agency long, get supervisor positions became frustrating and overwhelming.

I started to question my ability to lead in the field of social work. Was this as far as I was supposed to go? Would this be the next 30 years of my life? These questions were perpetually running through my mind, and this was the start of my routine negative self-talk regarding my skills and abilities in the professional world. I eventually resigned myself to limits and invisible ceilings. I was becoming my own worst enemy.

I can remember vividly pulling into the parking lot of my job and having trouble getting out the car to walk into the building. Not due to any physical condition, but as a result of frustration over working hard and investing into an agency that didn't see my true value. I started experiencing these feelings often and realized I was moving from unhappy to situationally depressed.

This turmoil started to spill over into my personal life. I began leaving work, stopping by my favorite neighborhood restaurant for dinner, going home to a glass of wine and tucking myself in bed by 8 p.m. My social interactions shriveled to nothing, and my weekends were spent watching television reruns. This was my routine for months. I felt like I was standing outside of myself, watching life pass me by. I was miserable, and I realized I had to figure out how to pull myself out of this funk.

I decided to explore different and intricate details about my chosen profession. Learning new things was one of my happy places, and I realized that I had to experience small wins in any way possible. Opportunities to learn new skills in my child protective services social work position were limited, so I began researching other ways that social workers served citizens, including youths, in my city.

I discovered that I could be a provider of the services and programs to which I was currently referring my clients. I went to my supervisor to ask that I be allowed to offer parent education support to one of my clients, who because of economic reasons did not have the resources to attend the required parenting classes. I was told that I was not qualified to provide parenting education, and that I needed to stay in my lane.

That day changed everything. I altered my after-work routine, and instead of dining and going straight to bed, I spent several hours researching various social work roles. After accepting that what was limiting my success was the lack of necessary credentialing, I made up my mind to do something about it. If I needed to become a licensed clinical social worker to move to the next level, I would. Although it was cloudy, the vision was there. I didn't know what the end result was going to be, but I knew it was time to move forward and continue my education.

Going to work was now different, because I had a purpose. I changed how I viewed my position; it was now a means to an end. I no longer saw my daily routine as something I would be doing until retirement; I viewed it as a form of stability that provided me with the opportunity to engage in the training needed to shift my skills to a more clinical focus.

For the next four years, I took advantage of the resources my position offered me without worrying about becoming a supervisor. My dreams had become larger than this space, and although I did not have all the pieces, the puzzle was fully forming in my head.

In 2010, the vision became clearer with the development of my business. During this time, my goal was little more than to have the ability to say, "I have a small private practice." Over the next three years I increased my clinical skills by working as a part-time outpatient therapist and leading a small team of mental health professionals. Gaining the realization that I had finally outgrown my position as a child welfare social worker, both personally and professionally, I made the decision to walk away.

The transition to seeing my private practice as a full-time job versus 'something on the side' was gratifying, but not always easy. Although I was fully operating as a clinical social worker and walking the path I had paved several years earlier, I was still experiencing the same kind of limited opportunities for growth and leadership I had dealt with in child welfare. Personal relationship decisions left me commuting from my home in South Carolina to North Carolina for about two years.

The end of this personal relationship afforded me a professional opportunity to live and work in the same location, and I was beyond excited. I finally landed a position that allowed me to work with a population I was truly passionate about serving. This was the start of a new and exciting journey — at least that's what I thought.

"Stand down until further notice" was the statement I received from my supervisor on a Monday morning while preparing to head to my new job. Within my workplace, this vernacular meant imminent termination. I steadied my emotions for what was to come; but honestly, I was not upset about having to 'stand down,' mainly because my excitement for this position had been short lived. I discovered soon after starting that I still would not be able to truly work in the clinical capacity that was my 'calling.' My heart no longer valued the position. I appreciated working with children, but I knew there was so much more I had to offer youths impacted by the field of social work.

Prior to standing down, I knew I was making poor decisions regarding my job. There were days I would leave early and other days I would not go in at all. I was working with children, yet feeling more like a camp counselor than a therapist.

I was miserable in the job as well as in my personal life. I was dealing with a breakup and health concerns, but my frustration was largely due to being a trained psychotherapist and credentialed play therapist and not having the ability to fully use my skills in the work setting. My aspirations were much higher than that job would allow. I only found joy in working when in the office of my private practice.

After a week of standing down, I was given the option to end my current contract or be placed for two weeks in an out-of-town assignment that would further distance me from using my clinical skillset and working with children. Either way, what I heard in these options was the human resources representative telling me I was fired.

Fired was not the language used in the conversation, but that was the feeling I walked away with. Although I was not meeting work expectations, I had never been fired from a job, and the reality of my decisions kicked in.

However, I decided this was the time to turn a negative into a positive and to fully pursue my dreams. My aspirations were much higher than that job, and being forced to step out on faith was the catalyst I needed to finally live up to them. During the next few weeks, I regained my independence, moved into a new apartment and moved my part-time private practice into a bigger location. I also decided to fold my private practice into a group practice.

With all of these shifts came the need for a steady source of income, until my entrepreneurial endeavors stabilized. Fear began to set in. I was flooded with negative thoughts about failing and being unable to maintain a stable practice. I was on my own, with only the words of my grandmother pressing me forward: "You become to help others become."

I often sat up at night, looking at other psychotherapists' Facebook pages and websites, getting upset when I noticed they were younger and more successful than me, based on their timelines. Every time I would tell myself I could do the same thing, my inner voice would wage battle, with negative declarations such as "You need to find a real job," and "Your business will never grow to that level," versus the encouraging words of my grandmother.

There were times when the negative won, and that inner voice prevented me from doing things like increasing my social media interactions and announcing that I was operating a full-time private practice, not to mention coming to a complete stop on signing a publishing contract for my first children's book, *No, No Elizabeth*, and moving forward with using illustrations to create products for what is now Focus on Feelings®, a line of multicultural products that help increase children's emotional intelligence that I had begun two years earlier.

The more I allowed fear, depression and anxiety to consume me, the harder it became for me to fully operate my business. For about seven months, I remained stuck in this cycle and eventually succumbing to binging on TV and refusing to leave my house. A close friend called me out of concern and asked a question that challenged me. What was I doing with my life?

The question made me think about what I really wanted — for my life and my career. One of my major complaints while working full-time had been not having the time to do what I really loved to do, such as building my business and expanding my brand. It was almost as if I was waiting on someone to do it for me. I had become complacent. But my friend's question jarred me back to reality. All great plans require an executioner. I had to be and do.

Although the opportunity was in place for me to build my business full-time, I still faced challenges. The negative thoughts and fears I carried had led me to make poor business decisions and miss opportunities that would have helped me reach my goals. I am a firm believer that our personal experiences and mental health challenges will show up in our professional lives. This includes our past traumas, our family narratives and the words we speak to ourselves. This was the case with me.

Asking for help was a challenge for me, and I would often get discouraged when reaching out for assistance or guidance and not receiving a positive response. I quickly learned, however, the power of community and the importance of networking and connecting with the right individuals. I learned that I could no longer move forward in business being isolated and not connected to the right support systems.

During this period I grew a lot, and I came away with the understanding that in seasons of stretching, you will often find yourself outgrowing people, places and things, needing to take certain journeys alone. This is not saying that you should end friendships and relationships; however, evaluating your relationships will be an important step in your continued growth, and in alleviating distractions. When I accepted these truths and began to implement them, my smaller network wound up being a more solid and supportive one — which was just what I needed to finally propel myself forward.

I allowed myself to step out of my own way. I began to take more professional risks — the kind that placed me in the forefront and spotlight. Making strong connections within my profession was beneficial to my personal and professional growth. My professional community opened doors to opportunities that would have taken me extended time to cultivate on my own and extensive resources to obtain. Although my plan was to connect more with like-minded professionals in the therapy world, I learned there was a greater need to connect with individuals in various business arenas.

I still remember, like it was yesterday, the conversation with my grandmother that would eventually sustain me during my darkest professional days. It had occurred during a holiday break while I was pursuing my undergraduate degree. My grandmother had declared: "You become to help others become. When you lose that, you will not grow."

That statement resonates with me even today and has assisted me in the development of my therapy practice motto: "I Grow, You Grow, Together We Will Grow." The concept of "Together We Will Grow" is the driving force behind how I lead and the way I show up for others, in both my personal and professional life.

As a psychotherapist, my goal is to hold space for people to work on their personal goals related to their emotional wellbeing. As a leader within the field of social work and of my business, my goal is to share my knowledge and skills with others to help with their growth and to prevent them from having the same experiences I faced when I was trying to identify a professional path.

I have learned over my career the importance of striving and moving with a clear understanding of your purpose — your why. I've also learned that when things appear to be falling apart, they often are actually falling together.

As I grow, you grow, and together we will G.R.O.W

G: *Going away* from societal expectations that have you trapped in a profession or position you no longer find fulfilling.

R: *Recognizing the strongholds* that are preventing you from moving forward with your goals and dreams.

O: *Overcoming both external and self-created obstacles* that are in your path of growth.

W: *Working to your full potential* to reach and maintain your goals.

#BillableHours

By Kimberly Lawson

While growing up in Sylvester, Georgia, a tiny farming community in the southwestern part of the state, I was raised to believe that family comes before business. As a result, I've always felt obligated to offer services to family, and to friends of my family, at a deep discount or free of charge.

Looking back on it now and recalling all of the services I gave away blows my mind! And while I've since put better boundaries and business protocols in place, I have no regrets, because I did what felt right in my heart at that time.

My mom's side of the family is extremely small, and during my formative years in Sylvester, Georgia, I primarily spent my weekends and holidays with those relatives, including Gerard (or Rod, as his mom called him), a first cousin who was six months younger than me. My life and Gerard's were extremely intertwined, as we were in the same grade, both participated in band, had the same first job and even the same kind of first car. Not to mention that we were also neighbors! Growing up this close to a family member was a nightmare when I was young, but the more we matured, the more we appreciated the special bond we shared.

I was a Southern Belle in every sense of the phrase; but Gerard always had dreams of grandeur, and Sylvester was always too small for him. Though I never felt like I fit in this small town, I still loved living there. It was like the television show *Cheers — where "...everybody knows your name...and they're always glad you came."*

When I was a sophomore in high school, a longtime family friend came to my dad and asked for help with acquiring a government contract to do all of the landscaping for our small town. My dad informed him that his proposal sounded good verbally, but needed to look more professional on paper.

This gentleman knew I was a good writer and did well in school, so when my dad suggested that I could help him, he loved the idea. Even at that young age, I wanted to see my people (family and friends) succeed, so I agreed.

Being fifteen or sixteen at the time, I had no idea about the amount of work preparing a landscaping bid would require. For four days, I spent three to four hours after school sitting in front of the computer, typing his handwritten proposal, checking grammar, and ensuring that all required portions were included. At the last minute, we (the family friend and I) received notice that a critical component was missing from the proposal; therefore, I spent three hours before school finishing up this important task — one that could drastically alter his business model and change his life for the better.

In the end, the family friend won the bid and has been fulfilling this lucrative contract with this city for more than twenty years. By now, he has made well over six figures; however, I was paid $50 for all of my hard work. The service I offered was valuable. Yet, I didn't see my worth because I was not comfortable separating personal business from "business business."

To be transparent, I didn't even charge the family friend $50. When he asked how much he owed, I said $20. Because he realized that I spent several days completing the task — and missed a half day of school — he deemed $50 was fair, and I happily accepted.

He was practically family, right? It was my responsibility to make sure he did, well right? Family takes care of family, right?

After we both graduated from college, Gerard knew he wanted to move to Atlanta and become a millionaire-celebrity. Yes, he wanted the money and the fame. Meanwhile, I simply wanted something more than what I grew up seeing; I just wasn't sure what that was yet.

When we entered our thirties, Gerard was bit by the entrepreneurial bug and started an entertainment company. However, I was still giving complimentary advice in some instances and undercharging for my services in others — whenever a family member or friend needed me. I was an English teacher, I had published two books and I was still writing resumes and proofreading others' work. Yet, I still did not view my skills as a service worth officially selling.

One of my roles in the family was to plan family events; so in 2015, I orchestrated our first reunion in almost ten years. I called Gerard and told him what I was doing and asked him to bring his DJ equipment so we could have music. Without hesitation, he declared that he only loads his DJ equipment if it is a paying gig. Without hesitation, I snapped back that I was never going to pay him to do something for his family.

We found ourselves at an impasse. Before ending the call,

Gerard calmly told me that I shouldn't take it personal, but his DJ equipment had to be saved for "billable hours." Gerard made it clear that he cherished family as much as me; he just had a clear distinction between family and business. His belief clashed with everything I took to heart about business and family, and this was one of the few things he and I disagreed about.

My parents split around this time and my mom continued living in the home I grew up in. She and I began discussing how she was going to keep the grass cut, because my dad had taken the lawn mower and my older brother lived hours away. I suggested that she call the family friend about cutting her grass, to which she responded that she was unsure if she could afford his fee. At that moment, the music stopped in my brain like a record being scratched. "He's going to charge you?" I mused. Wow, so the friend was comfortable charging family, too. What was my hang-up?

On April 9, 2018 around noon, Gerard posted on Facebook that he had launched a new website and invited everyone to check it out. Upon seeing the post, I immediately clicked on the link to take a look and show my support.

I noticed the home page included an introductory sentence that was slightly choppy, and I knew I could give Gerard a better opening sentence for his website. I jokingly said to myself that I would call him later and give him a better sentence and tell him that I would give him the sentence for free, which he should appreciate, being that he believed firmly in billable hours.

Sadly, I was never given that opportunity. That afternoon, Gerard died in his sleep. Needless to say, I was devastated, as was our entire family.

Throughout that next year, I thought about Gerard's belief about billable hours. I never understood why he would not DJ for his family for free. I also questioned whether my chosen profession of teaching was what I was supposed to be doing with my life. I had conversations in my head that I would have normally had with my best friend and confidante Gerard, but he was no longer here.

In April 2019, exactly a year after his death, my answer came one day as I sat at my desk, talking with a co-worker about him and peering at the last photo that he and I took together, at the family reunion in 2017. I told her there had to be a deeper meaning to his death, that I didn't believe God would break our hearts without there being a greater purpose. I recalled his unwillingness to DJ for free. Then the heavens opened and my cousin's spirit poured into me. Eureka! Billable hours!

In that moment, I realized that Gerard was not saying he did not value his family enough to bring his equipment and allow us to enjoy his services; he recognized that every time he offered his services for free he put his business in the red.

The family reunion was three hours away from his home. Once he loaded all of his equipment into his SUV, his wife and son would have to travel in a second vehicle. Then there was the time it would take to unload and load the equipment multiple times, before and after the event. Gerard knew his services were valuable, and that at the very least, he should be paid for his time. Reflecting back, I agreed, and I accepted what the universe was trying to tell me: I had been sitting on billable hours since I was thirteen.

Thinking about that now, I can only laugh and be thankful. I laugh at how naïve I was, and I am thankful for the lessons I learned from those experiences. Why did I believe I had to be a martyr for family and friends when it came to business affairs? Why was I so uncomfortable charging family and friends for services that they would gladly pay a non-family member or stranger for? Did my family not believe in me enough to pay for my services?

Gerard had discovered that government agencies, including schools, only do business with companies registered with the state. His DJ business began to boom after he legally organized his company, because he was able to reach a whole new market, providing services for school dances and for company functions. My reflections on his decision and the conversation we had about him establishing his LLC poured into my spirit to follow in his footsteps.

I grew confident in my stance that billable hours are not just for strangers. They are for family, too. Honestly, billable hours should apply moreso to family and friends than strangers. Family members and friends should want to support you by patronizing the business.

While I never personally cut my cousin a check for his entertainment business, I did refer every person I knew to him, and many of them did hire him. As they should have, because he was professional and extremely passionate about the services he provided. He was also very comfortable talking numbers with prospective clients. I finally realized that charging family and friends was a big deal because I made it a big deal.

In addition to helping a friend write a bid for a project, I was creating resumes for friends and family members. Once I became comfortable with charging anyone, including my grandmother, then it was no longer the elephant in the room. In order to maximize my billable hours, I finally launched my own company, Lawson

Learning Academy, and I haven't looked back.

Since my beloved Gerard poured so much into me, allow me to pour into you. The fact that you are reading this book tells me that you are an intelligent person who adds value to the world. This is my advice to you:

1. Value yourself more than anyone else values you. Gerard charged premium prices for his DJ services because he believed the experience he created was worth his fee. One of the services my company offers is resume creation and interview prep sessions. Over the years, I have created or revised hundreds of resumes, and over ninety percent of them have resulted in the person being hired for the job he or she desired. However, for every resume a client purchased, there were individuals who inquired about my services and said I was too expensive, even when I was charging only twenty dollars.

   This is totally okay, because not everyone who inquires about your services is your client. Additionally, by valuing my services, I no longer offer family and friends discounts on services, and I am never upset when anyone complains about my prices. There is a reason you never see commercials advertising Maseratis. By charging for your services you're stating two things: you recognize that there is a market for these services and that the services you are offering are adding value. Once you respect your services, your clientele will, too.

2. Legally organize your business. Many people do not take the extra step of legally organizing their businesses because they do not want to have to report the financial earnings to the state. However, taking this step to register your business with the state shows that you are serious and professional and should be treated as such.

3. Let your passion fuel you. If you're not passionate about the services and products you're selling, your business will suffer. Throughout my life, I've had many side hustles. I've sold Avon, Tupperware, Scentsy, Herbal Supplements and waist trainers. While I always made my money back from the initial investment, I was never able to turn the side hustle into a full-fledged business, because I lacked a passion for the business.

   Oprah has been quoted as saying that *"Passion is energy. Feel the power that comes from focusing on what excites you."* This is so true. I remember when my cousin Gerard and I discussed him starting the DJ business. I jokingly remarked that he had found a way to get paid to party. Reflecting on that conversation, it poured into my spirit why not? Why not get paid to do something you love? Why not find your passion and turn it into a business? Realizing that I have a passion for helping others turn their dreams into reality fuels my business.

4. Time to do your self-assessment and pull out your calculator: What service or product do you offer that family and

friends rave about? The one that your family members tell everyone you're great at and recommend that people have a conversation with you about? How many times have you offered those services for free or gave the product away without charging a fee? Add it all up, then multiply it by two, because you probably did not recall every instance. To be successful in business you have to be willing to invoice for your billable hours.

What have I learned on this entrepreneurial journey? That family can have a huge impact on your life, including when it comes to business. Without the influence of my family, and Gerard in particular, I probably would not be in business today. I am thankful for the multiple indirect lessons that my family poured into me. These lessons helped me find my passion and turn it into revenue. I challenge you to find the courage to do the same and turn your passion into billable hours.

Inspiring Through Styling

By Cynthia Campbell

Long before I opened a fashion boutique in 2012, I noticed how some women exhibited low self-esteem, whether it was about their hair, makeup, clothes or their size. That really bothered me, because I believed from a very young age that women are beautiful, no matter what they perceive as personal flaws.

When I was a little girl, I would watch my grandmother match her dresses and shoes, especially when it was time to go to church. She never wore pants, and her dresses were always so pretty. I would sneak into her closet and slip on her shoes, just to hear the sound of the heels when I walked. When pantyhose became popular, I encouraged her to start wearing them instead of her regular stockings, which were much less sheer and flexible. It was a challenge, but she finally agreed.

Being a teenager was exciting for me, especially when it was time to shop for school clothes, Christmas and other holidays. My mom would let me choose my siblings' clothes, and oh boy, I was like a kid in a candy store, picking out everything and putting the right colors together.

When it was time to shop for my mom, that was the icing on

the cake. Either her hats and dresses or shoes and handbags had to match, and it was exciting to find just the perfect items for her. She trusted me, and it was a pleasure to serve as her personal stylist. Those special moments of shopping were my first experiences with pouring into others in a way that also gave me joy. I found it to be a blessing to use fashion to help people see things differently.

Using that gift gave me the opportunity to help improve others' self-esteem, and as I grew older, I came to understand how important a role this was. Positive self-esteem can help you achieve a positive attitude and help you accomplish your goals.

I carried that belief with me well into adulthood, and it gave me an advantage during the 10 years I worked as a Certified Nursing Assistant. I enjoyed dressing my patients for special occasions.

I had always dreamed of operating my own fashion business, and in 2014, I took a leap of faith and opened a boutique in Rosedale, New York. I operated the business there for two years before closing it and focusing on mobile fashion opportunities, which meant I traveled to share my products with potential clients.

In 2017, I opened another fixed location, this time in Valley Stream, New York. I was nervous, because this boutique space was bigger than the first one, and the opportunity to move my business there happened so quickly. With encouragement from my family, however, and by focusing on all of the reasons this business mattered, I was able to move past my fears and move forward.

I realized that by expanding, I could help more customers feel like the Diva they deserved to be. Because along with enjoying the process of buying and stocking pretty things in my mobile store and fixed location, making customers feel good about trying on and buying certain styles of clothing was my purpose. I wanted each customer to look in the mirror, turn from side to side and feel comfortable with her true self. Even now, every time I see this happen, I am grateful.

One of my favorite ways of pouring into others is sharing my expertise when a client has an important event and is unsure of what to wear. This is when I pull out all the stops, whether it be casual or elegant. For a casual outing, I may suggest high-rise, low rise or boot cut denim jeans, pair them with a beautiful colorful top, and accent the look with earrings and a necklace to match. For elegant wear, I usually recommend stepping away from the black dress and going with a beautiful color that contours to the client's body. Pair this with the perfect jewelry, shoes and handbag and she will be ready.

My business, Emeirelle Boutique On Wheels, has really been a blessing, as it has allowed me to not only pour into others' lives, but also to pour into my own life numerous opportunities that might not otherwise have presented themselves, such as being able to host fashion shows on the road and serve as a personal shopper for some of my boutique clients.

I've learned through working to enhance others' self-esteem that I can do great things, too. When the ladies come to my boutique and love what they purchase, they leave happy, and I know I have given them lasting gifts.

Use Your Gifts Right Where You Are

By Edwinette Moses

In 1986, the Space Shuttle Challenger was on its maiden voyage with seven crew members aboard. Having excelled both educationally and professionally, anyone familiar with the tragedy that occurred would agree the crew members would undoubtedly have made major contributions in the fields of science and technology had they not taken that fateful flight. These astronauts, ages 35 to 46, had backgrounds in engineering, biomedical engineering and physics, and they seemed to have been born with an innate ability to succeed early in life. What was the driving force behind their success? When did they discover their purpose?

While few of us can claim to have personally known these astronauts, we likely can recall instances in which we have encountered or been inspired by people who have successful careers or profitable businesses or have contributed to society in some way. On our personal journeys to find meaning or meaningfulness in life, there is a tendency to measure our successes, or lack thereof, by what others have accomplished. We have a jaded view as we search for our own measure of status or success.

Television has brought the world into our homes and

sensationalized life and how we define success. For example, we're introduced to child prodigies who simply amaze everyone with their talents and skills by accomplishing great feats, like singing opera or playing concertos at young ages. Or, we've been mesmerized by orators like the Reverend Dr. Martin Luther King, Jr. and Malcom X, who delivered their messages with great passion and authority. They, too, seemed to have accomplished much early in life. But when does one know for sure where they belong?

Viktor Frankl, a prominent neurologist, psychiatrist, holocaust survivor and author, once theorized, "...mental health is based on a certain degree of tension, the tension between what one has already achieved and what one still has to accomplish...."

Throughout his book, *Man's Search for Meaning*, Frankl explores how one's life's purpose and meaning are not synonymous with happiness. We want overnight success, we want it our way and in our time. However, we cannot control our fate. Frankl helps us navigate through this reality by suggesting that "what man actually needs is not a tensionless state, but the striving and struggling for a worthwhile goal, a freely chosen task." In other words, trials make us stronger.

Although I should have known better, I often would try to measure up to others and send myself into a state of performance anxiety by asking so many questions, such as: *When will I find meaning? Where do I belong?"* According to the prestigious magazine *Harvard Business Review*, "a small number of people know very early where they belong. Mathematicians, musicians and cooks.... But most people, especially highly gifted people, do not really know where they belong until they are well past their mid twenties."

The vast majority of people will need to work hard to navigate the ebbs and flows of life until a breakthrough is achieved. Of course, I cannot compare myself to the mathematicians, musicians and certainly not a cook; neither do I consider myself "highly gifted." However, as the Holy Scriptures indicate in Ecclesiastes 3:1, *For everything there is a season, a time for every activity under heaven*, and somewhat late in life, I began to search for meaning.

In my late 30s there was an aha moment that opened my mind to better understanding that there was indeed a purpose for my existence, and I began to fully appreciate life on earth. *Why did it take so long?* In addition to navigating life itself, and experiencing what I now know as "degrees of tension," there was another barrier — religious doctrine. Above all else, religious teachings stunted my growth. Yes, it sounds a bit strange, but let me explain.

Growing up with a strict Pentecostal background was the driving force behind my strong belief system and approach to all things, both spiritual and secular. *How firm a foundation?* It was a firm foundation rooted in biblical truths supplemented by doctrines that were rules-based, and in reliance on personal experiences mixed with unwitting misinterpretation of scripture. What stunted me in every way was the notion that every 2,000 years there would be a change.

The last "change" was the birth of Jesus, and surely the next would be his return to rapture the church. I wanted to be ready! My hope was in a heavenly home, because earthly things would soon be gone. Really *soon*! Fast approaching was Y2K! We would joyously sing, *Soon, I will be done with the troubles of this world....* I didn't have long, so why should I worry about temporal things? It just wasn't worth it, based on what I was taught and deeply believed about the Bible and fulfillment of the prophecies.

Being surrounded by family and friends who held close those same values and principles kept me grounded and undefiled. Without having any outside influences — we didn't mingle with the "world" — I believed everything I was told and did my best to follow the rules.

My aha moment that life was not really going to be over arrived when 1999 ended at the stroke of midnight. We entered a year that was eerily similar to the 18th century period known as the Enlightenment, when individualism, reasoning, skepticism and intellectual movements flourished.

Now, I am definitely not skeptical with regard to my Christian faith, and I still hold fast today to my beliefs. However, after navigating life and its surprises, I began to examine my early religious influences and the associated fear and anxiety that, in essence, kept me from appreciating and using my God-given natural abilities. Thankfully, time can bring about growth and change, and while I still found my religious training relevant, I slowly began putting things into perspective and asking questions about the meaning of life.

This was a process. I navigated through my newly found ideals and curiosity in phases, while accepting that the end of the world was not imminent, and that I needed a path forward for living on earth instead of focusing on the journey to my heavenly kingdom. I had to figure out what I was living for and why, and what I wanted to do with my life.

After routinely asking these essential questions, I found myself floundering for answers. Everything I had accomplished or enjoyed up to this point had been connected to my church and my faith. Climbing the corporate ladder was a foreign concept; I was only familiar with watching close family and friends become leaders and receive promotions in religious settings. I wondered where or when I would get tapped for a role or position — that "what shall I render...what shall I give... message that was always preached. Surely my day would come.

Over time, I understood there was a need for my talents anywhere I was permitted to use them. It was a different viewpoint, but a real one. The proverbial dots were connecting that there are no limits unless we set them. I recalled the scriptures about enlarging our territories, doing all things through Christ and with God all things are possible. Here was my chance to move! I needed a new audience into which I could *pour*. I had accepted that moving on was not blasphemous or forsaking what I was taught; it was merely taking an opportunity to infuse others the way God planned it for me.

What I was not aware of was that the fabric of my entrepreneurial interests was being woven long before I embarked on this journey. As a child, I had watched my father, a World War II Veteran, work hard to provide for his family. He was a postal worker and had a side job working as what is known today as a landscaper for several wealthy families. Although these jobs were not rated as highly as some professions, his income kept us in what was then called middle class.

In addition to his secular jobs, he served as both a minister and deacon in church. During many years of dedicated service, his role expanded to community volunteer, including stints of service at the local food bank, where he sought to help the less fortunate. Dealing with people, regardless of their economic status or influence, takes a special person and talent, and what inspired me most was that my father could transition with ease between the well-to-do and the least of them. Reflecting on these memories afforded me the opportunity to further put things into perspective. I was encouraged that I would find my place!

Years later, my husband and I embarked on a journey that included renovating homes. This was nothing we intentionally set out to do; an opportunity was presented and we thought it was worth exploring. In the "good old days" houses were considered an appreciating asset, meaning the value of a home would always go up, while cars, for example, were depreciating assets, and values would go down immediately after driving off the car lot. This opportunity became available when the real estate market was pretty flat, meaning it was a buyer's market.

Of course, with every new venture there is some level of risk, be it the final decision to launch an idea or follow a dream, trade-offs in relationships or financial risks. Quite naturally, my husband and I were nervous about purchasing the home, because there was a chance it would not yield a return on investment. We anticipated some profit, but there was no guarantee that monies spent to renovate the home would be recovered when the house sold. We decided that since this property would be our first venture into real estate investing, we would be happy to break even at closing.

The period of time between purchasing, renovating and selling the property was approximately ninety days. This was remarkable for first-time investors during the early 2000s. Fortunately, all the boxes were checked and there was a small profit, a return on the investment that allowed us to pay off some personal debt. This venture turned out to be a positive introduction into the investor's market. However, a few months later, the housing market changed drastically. Homes in the area became a hot commodity and began to sell for more than three times the amount we settled on. This made us aware that timing is key. Just three or four months later, we could have made so much more money.

As time moved on, we began to acquire other properties. Some homes were sold and others kept as rental properties. In all cases, the properties needed to be completely rehabilitated, so we began purchasing home improvement items. These items included carpet, flooring, cabinetry, appliances and tools, to name a few. We kept amassing items and eventually realized things were slightly out of control.

As people of faith, we believe in the overflow and saw it unfold before our eyes. First, the garage became packed, and there was only a path to and from the garage to the kitchen door. More space was needed and we rented a storage unit. Rental box trucks would be used to haul items to the flea market where customers would be lined up waiting to see what items were available. The truck would first be loaded at the house, and then driven to the storage unit to get additional items. Whatever remained had to be taken back to storage or placed in the garage.

In fact, there was such an overflow that my husband began to employ young men to help with selling the overstock at the local flea market on Saturdays. Eventually, the guys needed to increase the flea market run to twice weekly, and they sold home improvement items on both Saturdays and Sundays. After approximately four years, those weekly runs to the flea market had become a bit overwhelming and it became apparent there had to be a better alternative.

In 2010, I finally got fed up with not being able to use my garage as it was intended. My husband gave me a charge — "You can look for a building" — so that is what I did. I needed to find a building large enough to consolidate the items in both my garage and the storage unit into a single place that was close to our home.

During the same period, I had made a few efforts to fulfill some heartfelt passions, including volunteering to help the less fortunate and starting my own business. While continuing to work my full-time job, I opened a health information management (HIM) consultant business, providing medical coding and reimbursement services to small medical practices. This business required a lot of onsite meetings and training sessions with employees and contract staff at the practices. While it was a great experience, the work was draining and underwhelming and required a lot of long hours. When I was forced to hire additional staff to fully leverage the business, I knew it was time to change course.

There were so many competing priorities that I had to place my soul-searching on hold. I made the shift to supporting my husband's endeavors, or should I say trying to get back into my garage. During this time, the country was in the middle of an economic recession, yet we continued to move forward. I located a building close to home that would meet the requirements and that was large enough to store all of the items we had on hand. Interestingly, this find was the beginning of an entirely new venture. Why not use the storage space as our own "store"?

In keeping with the flea market concept, we decided that business hours would be set and honored for Saturdays only. This would allow us to sustain the teams of family and friends who had been supportive during the flea market years. However, there continued to be overflow and an overstock of home improvement items. More opportunities became available and we expanded to an online store. A separate location was needed for shipping items to customers who did not live in close proximity to our brick and mortar "store," so we searched for a second location – this time, a warehouse, which we called the Station.

With the exception of the administrative setup of the store and warehouse, much of this venture was the brainchild of my husband. I was in someone else's shadow! Now well into my 40s, I was thinking, "I'm *all* the way behind. *Where do I belong? What will be my claim to fame?*" I was still searching, because I had put my quest for meaning on hold.

Approximately four years later, I had the pleasure of hearing one of my nieces express her feelings about me. This conversation gave me pause, as this was authentic feedback that offered answers to some of those thought-provoking questions I had been wrestling with for a while. She said I treated her lovingly, just as if she was my daughter, and that she appreciated the things I had shared with her over many years. Since then, others have shared compliments and accolades; however, there is always one word or deed that can close the deal. This was it!

What a revelation! I *am* where I belong, I realized! Once I began to embrace where I was and what I could do, my perspective changed. Over time, I had given little credence to my efforts, but all the while, I was making a difference — I was able to *pour* despite my perceived delays and lack of confidence in my abilities. Every perceived delay, it turns out, was a part of the plan.

For the past ten years, I have been able to provide jobs to family and friends. Specifically, the business was a bridge for some in difficult times — from the beginning we paid everyone who worked with us. Early on, I especially worked with teenage family members, offering most their first jobs as cashiers. They learned the fundamentals of conducting basic cash and check transaction, customer service skills, and pricing and stocking inventory. Everything I had been searching for was finally front-and-center: I was *overlooking* whatever it was I had been searching for and wanting to accomplish all along!

In short, sooner or later we will all find our place, where we belong. I submit that the "gaps" — those "degrees of tension" discussed by Frankl — keep success in rotation, so that everyone gets his turn. Consider how first responders during 911 and during the COVID—19 pandemic and the three women in the 2016 movie "Hidden Figures" are all examples of game changers — people who may not have necessarily been in the forefront early on, but became a source of inspiration for so many. For me, I was fortunate to realize success in unexpected places — in my family, place of employment, businesses and education — all areas into which I have poured freely and with gratitude.

Get Your Mind Right

By Eulica Kimber

W hat if I told you I have an investment opportunity that pays big dividends, without requiring a ton of money? What if I declared that the more you invest the more it grows, with the only requirement being that you actively participate, not sit on the sidelines, waiting on someone else to do the work for you? Would you invest? What is this opportunity, you ask? *Mindset.*

Did you know that mindset is the greatest gateway — or barrier — to success in any area of your life? You may not be aware that you have an issue with your mindset; but if you can identify with any of the following, you may want to take some time to self-examine and reset:

- Do you tend to eagerly push yourself to try new things and develop new skills? Are you open to new ideas?
- Or do you tend to stick with what is safe? Do you often resist or dismiss new information?

These questions give you an indication of what kind of mindset you possess, and that mindset gives you a view of the world around you and your place in it.

Have you ever been to a conference, read a book or took a class that taught you a lot, but nothing really changed in your life, business or habits? That may be a sign of your mindset. You may hear new information, yet be resistant to considering or applying that information to develop your perspective on a given subject, even if you NEED this information to meet your goal.

Or, your mindset may reveal itself by showing up as vague, undeveloped plans for your business or career. You start a venture, but never deep dive into the various tasks that would broaden your understanding and experience in a manner that helps you achieve your goals.

Here is an example of what I mean: One recent evening, I was having a Facebook Messenger (email) conversation with a budding entrepreneur who was seeking to start a travel business by joining a multi-level marketing organization. She was very argumentative as I asked probing questions about her vision and goals for her business.

I wanted to know how she would set herself apart from others in the same space. Her only response was that she was getting training from the person who recruited her and that money would flow. I continued to press by asking her about her target demographic and how she would reach them. She had no answer, but believed that somehow she would become wealthy and be able to retire early from her earnings.

I'll pause here to add some context to this story. At the time that conversation occurred, the world was experiencing the global health pandemic known as COVID-19, which had led to various shelter-in-place orders and business closures – in particular for the travel industry. With this at the top of my mind, I wanted to interrupt her and ask, "Girl, what the heck are you doing?"

As a business consultant, I wanted to know how she ended up joining the business at this time and how she was going to navigate during the unique economic climate. Let's just say the conversation didn't end well, and it turns out that she hadn't found her way to my DMs to ask for advice, but to instead invite me to a call to potentially join her team. She wanted no feedback and had done no market research; but made an investment to join the business based on a vague promise of wealth.

I begin with this story because it is not an uncommon conversation for me. Usually, I like to turn the topic to the potential client's passions, skills and abilities that can be leveraged into a profitable business. My methodology works with some people, but it used to frustrate me (still does) when I couldn't make a tangible impact in the lives of every entrepreneur I encountered. That was until I found out what separates wildly profitable people from others. It is MINDSET.

In her thirty years of research, Dr. Carol S. Dweck identifies two mindsets which affect the way we lead every area of our lives. Whichever you choose, that particular mindset impacts the way you show up in the world.

Those who possess a *fixed mindset* have a fixed level of core intelligence, personality and character which cannot be developed or built upon. Folks with a fixed mindset rarely excel because they are unable to push beyond the judgmental message of past failures. They may believe that others are just lucky or have a certain "it" factor for success; therefore, they give up on the journey and rarely reach major levels of success with any kind of consistency.

In contrast, those who possess the *growth mindset* believe that their core qualities can be cultivated and developed to deliver better results in every area of their lives. People with this mindset believe that talent is a result of effort. They are the people who come to conferences, read articles or tackle other kinds of learning opportunities with an open mind, seeking nuggets of wisdom to implement. Growth mindset people believe that their true potential is unknown, and they dedicate themselves to lifelong personal and professional development. They see failure and setbacks as a necessary part of the growth process.

Mindsets are formed and reinforced during our childhood, through praise and labeling. Parents and teachers often give feedback on what is acceptable based on ability or effort. Dr. Dweck found that those who were primarily praised for ability, test scores and grades began to reject new challenges that would expose their flaws. However, those who were praised for their efforts — meaning they were consistently told that their test scores or grades were merely a reflection of their hard work or persistence — learned to enjoy the process of problem solving and sought out new challenges.

Dr. Dweck cites several examples of what she calls the mindset of a champion. Champions like famed boxer Muhammad Ali are perfect case studies of the growth mindset. Not only did he speak what he envisioned, he also put in the work that would lead to his ultimate victory. One who possesses the growth mindset must be in it for the long haul. There are no easy wins; no quick wins. The public persona of Muhammad Ali was the words he spoke to his opponents. But I challenge you to recognize that those words were simply a manifestation of the hours of work, blood, sweat and tears that he invested in his training.

Remember, possessing a growth mindset is about having the courage to explore and expand the horizons of your capabilities and viewing limitations as opportunities to learn and grow. Many times we are afraid to explore because we are afraid to fail or we fear judgment. Those with a growth mindset consider their failures to be necessary lessons on the developmental path to success.

As a business consultant, I find it very challenging to coach anyone who does not have a growth mindset. I'm sure if you are a teacher, trainer or coach of any kind, you probably have had the same experience. The student with the brightest mind is not always the one who excels. Likewise, the business owner with the best idea is not always the one who prospers. What is the difference, you ask? Mindset! A fixed mindset will cause you to limit your business potential, and even your career explorations and earning potential.

Back to my story about the young lady who was starting the travel business. I wanted to talk with her about all of the possibilities she could explore with travel. I wanted to ask if she was going to lead guided tours, educational trips or even Mommy getaways. I wanted to know if, even inside of the multi-level marketing business model she was entering, she was willing to set herself apart, so that her business could stand out as distinct and desirable. I was disturbed that she would not even entertain a conversation to discuss new ideas.

The mind is a powerful and mysterious tool — specifically the power of your mindset. The good news, according to Dr. Dweck's research, is that the fence of fixed mindset can be removed with some investment of courage and effort. Yes, you have a choice. You can get your mind right!

My challenge to you is to make a decision to get your *"Get Your Mind Right"* — or at least get it moving in the right direction. Dr. Dweck found in her work that just learning about the growth mindset can cause major shifts in how people view themselves and the possibilities for their lives. You've now taken that step, and I have a few more suggestions for how to keep moving forward:

> ***Self-reflect and own what you see.*** I've found in my personal life and work that I cannot effectively pour into others what I do not possess myself. My mind has to be open to possibilities for myself and for those I serve. It took some time for me to arrive at this place of healing and wholeness; but I realized that in order to reach new levels of success, I needed to dig deep and understand the limitations I had placed on myself. I had to revisit painful situations in my childhood when I might have been told that I wasn't good enough or wasn't smart enough or pretty enough. As you do your own self-assessment, fill in your "blank" enoughs here. Sometimes these experiences can limit our thinking and shape the mindset from which we view the world.

> To be a good leader in business and life — that is, to be able to connect with and serve others — you must first be a good human, or a whole human. And when I say whole, I mean you must be unbroken by, or healed from, difficult life experiences.

You must be unbothered by whatever challenges the future may hold. Be honest with yourself about where you are and why you do the things that you do. Are you defensive when you meet sisters whose skillset exceeds yours? Are you truly happy for those who prosper around you? Are you honest about your shortcomings and able to seek and readily receive additional knowledge where needed?

I did this self-reflection in my life around motive. What was my motive for running an accounting firm? After some time, I realized that my accomplishments served as band-aids for the rejection I had experienced in my early life. I realized that I wasn't pouring into others out of my fullness. This meant I had to go down deep to really address some of those root issues. I had to forgive some folks and cry some (okay, a lot). This also meant that I had to be open to receiving counseling from a licensed therapist.

The experience was transformational. I came out on the other side determined to stop running my accounting firm like every other CPA. I became comfortable with my own story and grew to understand what I wanted to pour into others. So, I transitioned my business from a traditional accounting and tax practice into a planning and forward-thinking business-building practice. And for those who work with me, mindset is one of the first pillars we cover.

Never Graduate from Learning. When I say become a student, I don't just mean obtaining certificates and degrees. What I mean is become truly invested in building your mind, strengthening your body and developing your abilities. I want you to become excited about your personal growth, understanding that you are the greatest investment that will prosper you.

Some things you learn may be within an actual program, while other growth opportunities may happen in conversations with a mentor or expert in a certain field. It may be that you should invest in a coach or someone else who has "been there and done that" in the area in which you want to grow. It may mean that you go to a conference or workshop, but this time with tangible, actionable outcomes instead of leaving exactly the same way you came. With a teachable mindset, you'll finish each learning opportunity with your fountain a little fuller every time!

Cultivate Your Squad. The company you keep impacts your conversations, habits and the longterm outcomes of your life. In a 2008 article, David Burkus stated the following: "Your friends really are your future. And the implication is that you don't just need to be more deliberate about who you're spending the most time with. You need to be examining your entire network and its influence on your life. You need to know where you sit inside the larger network of your social community."

If you are going to truly live and thrive in this growth mindset lifestyle, you have to start running with people with the same mindset. I am not telling you to cut off everyone else, but you must begin cultivating your circles. These may actually be people you know; but this also includes the Facebook groups and other social media pages you follow. Your collective squad of voices should be speaking the language of the growth mindset.

So, what is on your mind and in your mindset? Prepare to go to the next level with both, so that when you enter into, or continue your journey in the world of business, you are pouring from a full fountain. You can only do that when you've invested in yourself. Become growth-minded and soon enough, potential clients will realize that you have the substance to meet their needs, while flourishing at meeting your own.

Strength, Courage and Wisdom

By Lisa F. Williams

A great debate continues to rage among scholars and theologians about whether leaders are born or made. Some may argue the point; however, it is my belief that all humans are freely given gifts and talents. We are created in the image and likeness of God the Father; so everything on the inside of Him was placed on the inside of us. He's in our DNA.

As I sat down to begin writing this chapter, I heard the words of India Arie's song *Strength Courage and Wisdom* in my ear:

> Always putting off my living for tomorrow,
> It's time to step out on faith.
> I've got to show my faith.
> It's been illusive for so long, but freedom is mine today.
> I've got to step out on faith. It's time to show my faith. Procrastination had me down, but look what I have found: I found Strength, Courage, and Wisdom,
> and it's been inside of me all along.
>
> (Arie, 2001, Track #4)

Strength

I can remember my mother telling me as a young girl, "You have to be a strong woman to compete in a man's world." This stuck with me throughout my life; and even now as a mature woman, I find myself encouraging and motivating others in a similar fashion – debunking the myth that women have been told for years, that we are the weaker sex and that our place is in the kitchen. I have never been interested in being offered a seat at the table. In fact, I create room for myself at the table.

You see, people will treat you the way that you present yourself. If you show them weakness, they will take that and use it to their advantage. I don't know any CEO who wants to work with weak individuals. They are looking for great leaders.

When I refer to strength, I'm speaking of intellectual strength, strength in the marketplace, strength in your character and strength in your stance. Mean what you say and say what you mean. As women and as leaders, we must demonstrate a sense of strength, even if it is at our own expense. I am not saying go out and compete head on with your male counterparts. However, you must be one step ahead of the competition; you must think strategically. You might have to put in late hours and take on projects that are outside of your scope of work or above your pay grade.

Over the course of my management career, I've learned that great leaders seek to strengthen their intellectual thinking through formal education or professional development opportunities. You won't find great leaders spending all day on Facebook; they are somewhere reading a book, taking a class, sitting in a seminar or learning from other thought leaders. The time is now for us to strengthen ourselves so that we can strengthen our young girls and young women. We need to let the younger generation know that they are the leaders of tomorrow; that there is more to life than posting half-nude pictures on social media or shooting videos that, later in life, they may regret. Somebody must tell them that everything they need for success is already inside of them. In many cases, all they need is someone to cultivate and mentor them, to show them how to dream bigger and shatter whatever glass ceilings are in their way.

Courage

The common definition of the word courage is "the ability to do something that frightens you." Simply stated, courage is commonly defined as being motivated from the heart to do something brave. The Bible defines courage as relying upon the supernatural power of God to be by your side. "Be strong and of good courage, do not fear nor be afraid of them; for the Lord your God, He is the One who goes with you. He will not leave you nor forsake you." (Deuteronomy 31:6) I can attribute much of my success in life to being mentored by dynamic leaders — male and female, inside and outside the church, including thought leaders I've admired from afar. However, knowing that God is by my side has made all the difference.

Perhaps the most powerful dimension of courage is that it is "personal, individual; someone ultimately acts alone even if others agree with the courageous act and regardless of whether it does or does not fit prevailing ethical narratives," declares P.B. Kritek in a paper titled "Reflections On Moral Courage" that was published in a 2017 issue of *Nursing Science Quarterly*.

In my work as a senior manager, I've come to understand that many things in leadership are taught, but much of a leader's success is caught. I've often wondered if that was where the quote "Give a man a fish and you feed him for a day; teach a man to fish and you feed him for a lifetime" came from. I digress! One must have the tenacity to take a chance. You have to do it afraid, whatever your "it" is. You have to stop living in your comfort zone; it's time to take off that robe and slipper and put on some running shoes. God has you covered, for he says in his Word: "I know the plans that I have for you, to prosper you and bring you to an expected end." So what are you afraid of?

Wisdom

Wisdom, from my perspective, is having experience, knowledge and good judgment. To label a choice as 'wise' implies that the action or inaction taken by a leader is strategically correct and timely. To acknowledge wisdom is also to acknowledge consequences for unwise or foolish choices.

A wise decision must be made with as much information as is available. To act wisely, an innovative leader must plan for what is a reasonable future situation, desire the outcome to be broadly beneficial, and then act. Author and former military leader Robert F. Dees writes in his book *Resilient Leaders: The Resilience Trilogy*: "It is empowering when leaders recognize they are inadequate for the task, allowing them to discard a façade of perfection and enabling their transparency as a leader."

The transparent leader will solicit employees' ideas without any form of self-censorship, so that over time, employees view the leader as a credible source with whom to give input and offer feedback, say Zhou, Cheng, and Xia in a 2014 issue of *Social Behavior and Personality: An International Journal* (Vol 42). In addition, leaders' "demonstrations of authentic and innovative behaviors set them up as role models to be imitated, and through these behaviors the leaders gain reciprocity from employees in the way of persistent attention to innovation," declare writers Weischer, Weibler, & Petersen in a 2013 *Leadership Quarterly* article.

Wisdom is the way we incorporate our values into our decision-making process, Wisdom is a gift given by God to anyone that asks for it. "If any of you lack wisdom, let him ask of God, that giveth to all men liberally, and upbraideth not; and it shall be given him." (James 1:5-6) God's wisdom is not just reserved for complicated situations. God's wisdom allows you to see beyond what might be standing right in front of you.

I shared this truth one day with a young woman who works with me. I told her that I saw so much in her, just waiting to come out. "You are the stabilizing force for your entire family," I said to her. "Do you want to do something different with your life? Or do you just want to continue working paycheck to paycheck?"

Even as I asked, I realized that she needed someone to walk with her and mentor her, because she couldn't "see the forest for the trees." I stepped up to the challenge, and the first thing I encouraged her to do was to quit her second job. Why? It was causing her to fall asleep at the main job — the one we worked together — and to slack off on her work to sneak to the bathroom to take a nap or talk on her cell phone to stay awake. She made it a common practice of appearing disheveled and tired. Many, including my manager, questioned why I did not just fire her. But I knew that she needed help, and finally I gave her this advice: "Write down your expenses. Then come up with an hourly rate that you would need to make in order to cover those expenses and let me know. I will see what I can do to get you to where you need to be."

Because she had an open heart and she was willing to listen, she grew. She was like a sponge, grasping hold to everything that I said, everything that I taught her and every class, training or book I suggested to her. In less than a year, I was able to promote her to Team Lead and in the process, increase her pay.

Even to this day, I continue to push her, and she continues to soak in the wisdom I share. I force her to apply for positions that I know will challenge her and test her skills. She takes everything in stride, and I can clearly see that she is going to be a great leader. She is married, with two lovely children, she purchased a brand-new house and that same year she brought a brand-new truck.

I do not take credit for any of this, God gets all the glory for giving me the wisdom in how to deal with not only this situation, but every situation that I encounter.

The goal of every great leader should be to develop people who will grow to do more or even greater than them. Leading in a way that helps others unleash what has been inside of them all along is rewarding. Having the opportunity to Pour into others should be every leader's goal!

Your Presence Matters

By Sharvette Mitchell

The first time I remember "serving" in a real and consistent capacity was when I was around eight or nine years old. I was an usher at Hungary Road Baptist Church, which is located in the suburbs of Richmond, Virginia. Let me tell you — I was proud to do it!

Every Sunday morning and some Sunday afternoons, I stood at the front door of the sanctuary, and as members and visitors entered, I would take them to an available seat or pass them a church fan. Through the years, I participated in other ways too, including singing with the youth choir and attending Vacation Bible School and Sunday School.

Around age 15, I started attending another church, Jerusalem Holy Church, located in the southside of Richmond. You guessed it: I was an usher there as well! At age 21, I became a member of my current church, New Jerusalem International Christian Ministries. I have held numerous leadership roles in my church, but my role as an usher stayed with me until into my 40s. Yes, you read that correctly!

I remember ushering for a special service years ago when a friend of mine visited the church. She was in the gospel music and radio industry. Surprised to seeing me at my post, she asked, "You are an usher?"

Let me add commentary and color around her statement. At that time, I was hosting The Sharvette Mitchell Radio Show (which remains one of my current endeavors). This friend knew I had interviewed people like Bern Nadette Stanis, the actress who played Thelma on Good Times, and other notable individuals. My "side hustle" business, Mitchell Productions, LLC, which has now become my full-time empire, was up and running pretty well. So, I guess my friend assumed that being an "usher" and serving the congregation would be beneath me.

This is where we get things wrong in business and in leadership, both of which are really about serving our customers and pouring into our audience and tribe. Some people think that it is the other way around and that once a certain level is reached, others should pour into and serve us. Some business owners hear the word "serve" and that sounds like "free" or "not for profit." Let me be crystal clear: There is nothing wrong with serving... as business owners, we just serve at a profit.

I will spend this time with you (i.e., aspiring entrepreneurs, business owners and side hustlers), de-bunking any negative thought process you have around serving your audience. Instead, read on as I lift up the positive impacts you will see as you pour into your audience by showing up, being visible and providing what they want and need.

No one can do what you do, the way you do it! Remember, the earth is waiting for your solutions and gifts...

Let's get into it!

How can you pour into your target audience and yield reward-ing results? There is one main way to accomplish this: with your presence. As an online strategist who works with clients around their visibility in the market, I am always shouting from the rooftop to show up, be seen and be heard. This is uncomfortable for some people, and I have noticed that it is most uncomfortable for my clients who are female.

Somewhere along the way in our society, at least in the United States, women have been made to feel like they should not speak up on their own behalf. This transfers into our businesses and brands. We don't want to be seen as needy, begging or greedy. Yet, our male counterparts don't place that filter or constraint on their actions, their marketing or their branding.

For some people, this inability to hang out their shingle and shout "I am open" is all tied to fear. The fear of visibility, in particular, can be crippling. It can stagnate any business, vision or dream. It can hold you back from pouring into your customers and audience. The consequence is that the transformation that could have happened for customers will go unfulfilled, because of YOU... and there is a hole in the marketplace.

Now, I know that might sting, but it's all very true. So, from henceforth and forever more, I put a demand on YOU to show up and to pour into your audience.

Take a moment and breathe.

Alright! Let's talk about the HOW. I will cover four ways to be present, which will positively affect the bottom line of your busi-ness. #POUR

1. Social Media

I know, I know! You are singing the song Heard It All Before by Sunshine Anderson. I am not naive enough to think that you have not heard or have not been told to use social media to promote your business and personal brand. However, I start with social media because it is the lowest hanging fruit and it is where your clients, supporters and audience hang out. It is the quickest place to show up and be present on behalf of your brand, and, more importantly to serve your audience. Your position and posture on social media should be that of a leader, resource and expert in your industry. And I should point out that leaders always get paid more...

To get started, here is a daily, weekly and monthly checklist to help you build your presence on social media:

Daily Checklist

- Post once or twice daily on social media sites where your clients hang out
- Check and respond to direct messages and inboxes
- Respond to any mentions or tags of your brand or pages
- Reply to or acknowledge all comments on your posts
- If your post is shared, show that person some love

Weekly Checklist

- Share video content (more to come on this topic!)
- Engage with other Thought Leaders and their content

- Offer your services or products (this can be multiple times during the week)
- Engage in your top active groups
- Post content on theme days (i.e. #MotivationMonday, #TBT-ThrowBack Thursday and #FridayIntroductions)
- Boost posts or run ads

Monthly Checklist

- Update profile or cover images based on your promotions
- Update or tweak your BIO section and links to ensure that they are accurate
- Review which posts had the most engagement and response (rinse and repeat)
- Plan your upcoming social media posts based on upcoming promotions and launches

After reviewing these checklists, your anxiety level may be rising. But again, pause and breathe; because leveraging social media is necessary to amplify your presence. The good news is that there are tools and resources to help you stay consistent. I love PostPlanner. com to schedule re-occurring posts on Facebook and Twitter. You can also hire a virtual assistant or social media manger to support you in managing your online presence.

But here's what you can't outsource or delegate: YOU. As Wade Harman, content marketing director for Kats Botanicals said, "Businesses who put a human face to their brand are the ones doing the best on social media." You, my friend, are the human face... #POUR

2. Live Streaming

Considering that Facebook paid media companies $50 million to produce live videos for its platform, it's clear that live streaming is continuing to grow in popularity. Are you ready to incorporate it into your marketing strategy and pour into your audience? You absolutely should, because live video is the next best option to actually being "there" in person. Typically, sales are higher when people interact with you in person; so video increases your conversion of followers into paying customers.

Most importantly, live streaming allows for instant two-way communication in these internet streets! You get the opportunity to serve your audience in a way that overshadows anything else you can do on the internet.

In addition, there is software available that allows you to stream to multiple platforms simultaneously – increasing your reach in an efficient way. I am in love with StreamYard.com, a software that allows me to stream live video to my Facebook business page (Mitchell Productions), my Facebook group (HeyGirlHey.today), my Facebook personal page @sharvette, YouTube @sharvette, Periscope @sharvette and Twitter @sharvette, All. At. The. Same. Time.

Before I go skipping down the yellow brick road of live streaming, let me deal with some excuses (i.e., fears) that may be surfacing in your mind right now. "I am scared! I don't like how my voice sounds! My kids will make noise. I don't know what I am going to talk about... What if nobody watches?"

Fair enough! However, not good enough to avoid trying this important platform. Here are four tips to help you get over the fear of doing Facebook Live or trying live streaming on other platforms:

- **Write down your talking points** - Preparation increases confidence! It is okay to have notes in front of you to help you feel more prepared.
- **Focus on your product and do a demonstration** - Perhaps you can make the live stream about your product. Hold up the product, show how to use it or wear it. This takes the focus off of you.
- **Use the Facebook share screen option** - You can share your screen and show a PowerPoint presentation so that your face is not on camera at all. This is a great way to test out live streaming.
- **Get over yourself** – LOL! At the end of the day, you just need to get over yourself. The world is waiting for what you have... #POUR

Now that I have convinced you, I'm sure your next question is, "What do I talk about?"

Glad you asked! You may have heard (or viewed) live streams that use standard themes, such as taking viewers behind the scenes, giving tips, talking about product or service features, or showcasing an event. All of that is good; however, let me tell you the secret sauce: Deal with your audience's fears and insecurities through your lens as an expert about your industry or the services you offer and you'll have them hooked. For example, here are examples of live stream topics I have used when promoting my Virtual Product & Course Academy:

- Creating a course is too complicated and overwhelming
- I am scared to do live webinars
- I am not an expert- people will think I am a joke
- I don't know what I would teach
- I have an idea for a course but I don't know if it is a good idea for a course
- What would I charge for a course, ebook, MasterClass, etc?
- I don't have time to create a course
- What If I launch a course and no one buys it?
- I don't have a big following; can I still launch a course?

When you deal with the unspoken fears, you rise to the top as a leader in the eyes of your audience and potential customers. You get to really speak to their fears and reassure your audience that you are the one to help close the gap.

Just before you hit that "go live" button, here is a high-level agenda you can use for all of your live streams to help them move smoothly:

1. Introduce yourself (i.e., who you are, what you do or your elevator speech).
2. Share the topic of discussion, which also should be the title of the live stream.
3. Engage with a few viewers and commenters and call them out by name. Or, show the comment on the screen.
4. Encourage viewers to like and share the video.
5. Cover a few points of your topic.
6. Reintroduce yourself (i.e., for viewers who have just tuned

in.)

7. Engage with viewers and commenters and answer any questions.

8. Finish covering your topic and do a quick recap of points.

9. Give a call to action (i.e., visit my website, schedule a consultation, buy my product, get my free download, join my Facebook group, etc.)

3. Media Interviews

You are meant for the world to hear and see. One strategy to do that is to be showcased or featured in live or recorded interviews and podcasts.

As mentioned before, I have hosted an internet talk radio show since March 2008 that now airs on multiple live streaming platforms as well. I would love to have you listen and watch at www. Sharvette.com. On a weekly basis, I interview all kinds of dynamic business owners, with some celebrities sprinkled in the mix. There is one common factor between my very good interviews and other interviews: the guests come to POUR into the audience.

As you work on increasing your visibility and presence, having the opportunity to be interviewed on TV shows, radio shows, podcasts, video shows, Zoom, etc. will give you great exposure to other people's audiences. This becomes your opportunity to pour, while showcasing your services or products.

In addition, you'll benefit from the interviewer's brand serving as an endorsement of yours, whether direct or indirect. Typically, an interview is an exchange, a dance if you will, between you and the interviewer. The end result is that you get to showcase your expertise and pour into the audience. This establishes rapport and the audience is much more likely to seek out your product or service.

The next question may be, how do I get interviewed? In this age of new media, there are interview opportunities all up and down the timelines of your social media pages. Simply make a post that you are looking for interview opportunities. You can go in groups on social media and search for interview opportunities. Here's a pro tip for podcasts that you follow: Search iTunes for your favorite podcasts and reach out to the host about interview opportunities (check the Show Notes).

Now, I am assuming you have the visual brand elements in place and you are ready for media exposure. If not, check out my Platform Builder Program at www.PlatFormBuilder.biz to learn how I can help you properly prepare.

Okay, let's get you ready to serve up all of your delicious expertise to audiences around the world! Preparation increases confidence. Yes, I said this already, but it bears repeating!

BEFORE an Interview

- Confirm details, such as dates and time zones. I could share war stories here, but I will spare you and hold that for another book. This is a very simple step that can cause a huge debacle if you miss a LIVE interview because you had the wrong date or time zone. Trust me, you will look bad, not the host...

- Confirm the interview method. Is this a LIVE video or an audio recording only? You will need to prepare differently if you are going to be on video. Oh, by the way, even if you have an "in person" interview at a radio station, you may still be on live video stream.

- Prepare the host. Make sure the host has your most recent BIO, and you can even send potential or recommended interview questions in advance. Hosts often appreciate this help with prepping for your conversation.

- Promote the interview. The purpose of the interview is for you to pour into audiences; so help that along by sharing the details of how people can watch or listen to your interview.

DURING an interview

- Arrive early. Even if this is an online interview, logging on early will help ease your nerves.

- Be conversational. The best interviews are like a conversation that the audience just happens to listen in on. Be natural and use the host's name in your responses. The more interviews you do, the more comfortable you will become.

- Give a "call to action" and direct the audience somewhere. This can be your website, a landing page for a free offer or to a consultation sign-up form. If this is not allowed, the host will let you know!

 AFTER your interview

- Thank the host. The best way to do this is on social media. Tag him or her!

- Share the interview. In most cases, you will be able to share the interview so that those in your audience can experience it. This establishes credibility for you and your presence.

- Update your BIO and website. If the interview is with a notable media outlet, mention that media outlet in your BIO and add that media outlet's logo to your website in a section called, "As Seen On."

Let me affirm that your voice is needed and wanted in your industry. Quiet any inner voice that is telling you otherwise and #POUR.

4. Email Marketing

Can I ask you a few questions? When was the last time you checked your email? Better yet, how many times have you checked it today? How many of those emails are from brands and stores offering you products and services? Stop reading this book and go look up the number to that last question. I am serious!

I am positive that you will find several emails from various brands and stores giving you coupon codes, announcing new products or sharing tips and advice. They realize that email is one of the most direct communication channels with their customers. Email marketing is a perfect opportunity to #POUR into your audience.

Let me share with you my highest-rated email thus far. This email got the most responses and the most opens.

Email subject line: *Transparent moment*

Last week I was invited to participate in a video shoot for CEO Magazine led by Sharon Oliver. I accepted and prepared to show up for the video shoot on this past Saturday. I arrived with a few outfits, my hair in rollers and a clean face since there was a professional make up artist there.

As I quietly sat at Club CEO studios and observed the other ladies that were going to be in the video, I recognized a few things. They were all younger than me (I was probably twice their age) and they were all very thin and probably had done some modeling in the past.

Here comes the transparent moment... For a split second I almost backed out and was going to leave because I felt like I did not FIT in this look for the video.

But a quiet voice inside of me said..."You belong in every room you go in." So I got my make up done, fluffed out my pretty bouncy curls in my hair and actually had a pretty amazing time doing the video shoot.

I don't know if you have ever felt like you did not belong somewhere but I hope this letter encourages you and reaffirms that you absolutely belong there!

See you at the top,
Sharvette

What you probably noticed was that I did not actually sell anything in the email. I did not mention my services or an upcoming program which I often do in my emails. However, I took the opportunity to share how I was human and had some doubts. That resonated with my customers and email subscribers.

Email allows you to make a connection with your customers and audience in a more intimate way than social media or even video. As leaders and business owners, one of the keys to your overall marketing plan should be building, growing and nurturing your email list.

Not convinced yet? Here are some statistics.

According to Oberlo, a dropshipping ecommerce company, in 2019, global email users amounted to 3.9 billion users. They project that by 2023, this figure is set to grow to 4.3 billion users. That's half of the world's population.

In addition, Oberlo reports that 81% of small businesses still rely on email as their primary customer acquisition channel and 80% use email to retain customers. Your business can't afford to ignore a tool as valuable as email marketing.

Lastly Oberlo reported that when looking at the frequency with which consumers would like to receive brand emails, 49% (Statista, 2017) of consumers said that they would like to receive promotional emails from their favorite brands on a weekly basis. This email marketing statistic is especially handy when you're worrying about sending emails to your customers too often. Your audience likes to hear from you, and apparently, they're happy to hear from you via email!

Building your email list.

The first step in building an email list is to select an email marketing tool. This will allow you to collect emails that get added to a database and then you can create an email and send it to your entire database. There are tons of email marketing tools out there so don't get stuck on which is the BEST tool. Pick one and go! I personally use GetResponse but there are others such as MailChimp, MailerLite, ActiveCampign, Mad Mimi, Drip and the list goes on. You can always upgrade or move your list so just get started.

To get customers and potential customers to join your email list, you will need to entice them by giving them something of value in exchange for their email addresses. This is called an opt-in or lead magnet. If you sell physical products, for example, a coupon code for a discounted or complimentary item is appropriate. If you are a service-based business, the item of value you offer could be several things, such as:

- Coupon code (example: lawn care service or hair stylist)

- eBook (example: author or consultant)
- Digital journal or planner (example: life coach or therapist)
- PDF checklist (example: health coach or graphic designer)
- Audio-mp3 affirmations (example: holistic doctor or motivational speaker)
- Video series/training (example: accountant or business coach)
- Challenges (example: credit repair specialist)
- LIVE webinar (example: all industries)

There is no right or wrong answer here. Choose something that ties to your business, service or programs, then create it and serve it to your audience. Once you have determined what you are giving to your email subscribers, you will need to have a landing page created in your email marketing tool and/or have the email marketing tool integrated into your website to start collecting email addresses.

There is common consensus in the industry that, the "Money is in the LIST!" The statistics back this up, with every $1 you spend in email marketing yielding a $44 return, according to Creative Studio Web.

Nurturing your email list.

A lot of people do a good job of the first step - collecting email addresses. However, most are prone to drop the ball after that. If you already have an email list, when was the last time you sent them an email? I will wait...

The critical factor in email marketing is to actually send out emails! The emails should be issued with some level of frequency and consistency, so that you stay at the top of your audience's mind. According to MarketingSherpa, 72% of people prefer to receive promotional content through email, compared to 17% who prefer to receive it on social media. This means your email subscribers want your emails, and this is a way to serve your audience.

Perhaps you are not sure what to say to your email subscribers. Here is a high-level series of email prompts you can use to create emails that you send to your new email subscribers. Key point: You can automate this step by using what is called "auto responders" within your email marketing tool.

Email Series Prompts

Email #1 (Day 1)- Send an automated welcome email immediately when the subscriber joins your list. Provide access to your free opt in/lead magnet and also invite them to like your social media pages, join your Facebook group, schedule a free consultation or subscribe to your YouTube channel. THIS email will have the highest open rate so use it!

Email #2 (Day 2 or 3) - Remind the email subscriber about the free opt in and highlight a tip covered in the free opt in. Make sure your website address is in the email.

Email #3 (Day 4 or 5) - Get intimate with the email subscriber audience and share your personal journey and why you do the work you do or offer the services you offer.

Email #4 (Day 6 or 7) - Elaborate on a key point from the free opt in and start sharing ways the email subscribers can work with you that tie to the free opt in. If you offer free consultations, share that. If you have videos that relate to this topic, share links to those videos.

Email #5 (Day 8 or 9) - Share customer testimonials and directly offer your services, programs and products. You can add a limited time offer to create urgency.

Email #6 (Day 10 or 11) - Share frequently asked questions from previous customers, "how to" videos and directly sell your services, programs and products.

Email #7 (Day 12) - Share your final call to action and directly sell your services, programs or products.

This series will get you started but it does not stop here! You will have email series related to the launch of programs, new products or events. As a goal, communicate with your email list at least once per week.

Here's what I have personally found by creating and nurturing my email list: 75% of my NEW customers come from my email list. This is particularly true for service-based professionals. For product-based companies, you will find that your REPEAT customers will come from your email list. Giving to your email subscribers has the effect of putting money in your pocket.

Are you ready to conquer the world now?

I have covered four ways to be present and pour into your audience - by way of social media, live streaming, media interviews and email marketing.

Let me be very clear — as a business owner and leader, your presence is required, even when you aren't selling something. I tell clients in my Platform Builder Program that I do not coach them to do *booty call marketing* (excuse my French if that offends you). You might be wondering, what is booty call marketing? Glad you asked!

You may have experienced OR know someone who has a male or female friend who only shows up when they want SOMETHING. They call late at night and just happen to be in the area. They text randomly but never consistently. They only contact you when they want SOMETHING. They never just call to talk or have lunch that won't later lead to an indecent proposal.

That's how some business owners are with customers. They only send emails out when they are selling a new product or service. They never post on social media until their new book is out. They don't do Facebook Lives just to pour into the audience; only to SELL tickets to their next event.

Sure, you might see a positive impact from some of these activities, but you will see an overwhelming flow when you embed pouring into your audience into the culture of your brand.

Wondering if I think you're ready? Glad you asked! Yes, indeed.
#POUR

Epilogue

By Stacy Hawkins Adams

When one thinks of a vessel, what may come to mind is a vase into which water is poured or a bowl of some sort that holds an edible item. Or, maybe you're thinking bigger — envisioning a boat that one can board to travel from one shore to another.

What may not readily surface is the possibility that we humans are vessels, too. For whatever our life's path may hold, each of us, with our unique experiences, beliefs and values, will approach the situations we find ourselves in, or the opportunities presented to us, in distinctly unique ways — ways that are particular to all that has shaped us into who we have been and who we're becoming.

Someone else may come along at the same moment in time as you; yet, because of your differences in upbringing, education or worldview, that person will likely resolve an issue or respond to possibilities differently than you. And just as no two vases, bowls or boats bear the exact same design, neither will different people pour into a passion or career or other individuals in the exact same manner.

Indeed, as you have read in this anthology, every entrepreneur pours in her own way. There were no two chapters alike, right? Yet, each writer shared details about stretching and growing, and ultimately, about giving back, through her journey. What was just as impactful as how each writer made her "business moves" was her willingness to share vulnerable moments along with victories — to ensure that you and other readers stay focused and keep trying, until you achieve the vision you hold in your heart.

I hope you have been motivated and mentored to persist in pursuing your goals, so that when you stand in positions of strength and success, your vessel will overflow with enough wisdom and influence to share with others. May you POUR, so that those who follow you can also pour, and the cycle can be repeated, again and again, flowing from one unique vessel to another. This is how the world changes, business-wise and otherwise, through shared creativity and calling filling the marketplace and the world.

MEET THE AUTHORS

Wendy Lee

Chapter 1: Whole Vessels Hold More Water

"By people we are hurt, by people we are also healed" is the motto that fuels Wendy Lee's motivation in all she does. Arising from the ashes of fear, intimidation and depression she graces various platforms to share her life through comedic speaking. Captivating her audience with her unique story and mesmerizing them with her clever delivery, Wendy desires to spark thought that leads to actions that provoke lasting change. With over a decade in the comedy industry, Wendy Lee is just scratching the surface in a league all her own. She is a Lawrenceville, VA native presently residing in Petersburg, VA.

Visit: www.wendyleequietstorm.com

Maria Davis-Pierre

Chapter 2: How Impact Multiplies When Used For Good

Meet Maria Davis-Pierre, Founder and CEO of Autism in Black Inc., located in West Palm Beach, Florida. This organization aims to bring awareness to Autism Spectrum Disorder and reduce the stigma associated with the diagnosis in the black community.

As a licensed mental health therapist, Maria primarily works with parents to provide support through education and advocacy training. Her passion for working in the field stems from her personal journey with ASD when her daughter received the diagnosis at a very early age.

In addition to therapy, Maria dons many other titles including coach, speaker, advocate, and author. Her first published work, The Self-Care Affirmation Journal, is currently available for purchase on Amazon. Maria's unique approach to coaching and counseling exemplifies her drive and motivation toward greater acceptance and overcoming the barriers and personal struggles associated with raising a child on the spectrum.

Visit: www.autisminblack.org

Andrea Davis

Chapter 3: I Was Born For This

Andrea Davis is a Certified Professional Coach, author, and speaker. Prior to becoming a Coach, she served 35 years in the Federal Government as a Contracting Officer, overseeing large-scale contracts for the Department of Defense, General Services Administration, and NASA. Toward the end of her career, Andrea began to realize that she wasn't living the fullest life possible, so she transitioned into entrepreneurship where she now coaches women over 50.

As the owner of Next Season Strategies, LLC, Andrea is also a member of the International Coaching Federation (ICF) and certified as a Professional Coach by the Institute for Professional Excellence in Coaching (iPEC). She is a graduate of Fayetteville State University and received an MBA from Florida Institute of Technology.

Andrea has served in various church leadership and ministry positions for the past 20 years, and is the single mother of an adult son who she considers her biggest cheerleader and greatest teacher. She recently relocated from the Washington, DC metropolitan area to Charlotte, NC.

Visit: www.MsAndreaDavis.com

Carmen Jimenez-Pride

Chapter 4: Falling Together

Carmen Jimenez-Pride is the founder of Outspoken Counseling and Consulting, LLC, and Play Therapy with Carmen Inc. Carmen is a Licensed Clinical Social Worker, Registered Play Therapist, and Business Consultant. Carmen is a serial entrepreneur and award-winning best selling author. She is the creator of Focus on Feelings®, a diverse line of emotional literacy products.

Visit: www.outspokenllc.com

Kimberly Lawson

Chapter 5: #BillableHours

Kimberly (Sherrelle) Lawson is an International Best-Selling Author, Business Coach, Podcast Host, and Speaker with a vision to make this world a more positive place than when she first entered it. What started as penning short stories and poetry as a child, ultimately turned into authoring several books and launching her publishing company, Sherrelle Ink, LLC.

Armed with an unwavering entrepreneurial spirit and a passion for helping budding and novice entrepreneurs thrive, Kimberly's company, Lawson Learning Academy, LLC specializes in helping individuals turn their dreams of entrepreneurship into a thriving successful business.

Kimberly has successfully coached many individuals to achieve their business goals.

Visit: www.SherrelleInk.com | www.KimberlyLawson.net

Cynthia Marie Footman-Campbell

Chapter 6: Inspiring Through Styling

Cynthia Marie Footman-Campbell, affectionately known as (Cookie), is the proud owner of Emeirelle Boutique on Wheels. She has been in business for 11 years in Valley Stream, New York.

"Our boutique features one of a kind women's clothing, handbags, jewelry, glasses, and many other accessories carefully-curated with you in mind. We only carry a few of each item, so everything you find is uniquely yours."

Cookie is a mom of 3 Children: Ericka 40, Kristopher 36, and Jessika 30. She has 9 grandchildren and is married to Edward Campbell.

Visit: www.emeirelleboutiqueny.com

Edwinette Moses

Chapter 7: Use Your Gifts Right Where You Are

A native of Richmond, Virginia, Edwinette earned her Bachelor of Arts in Liberal Arts from University of Richmond and Health Records Technician Certification from J.S. Reynolds Community College. She is employed with Veterans Health Administration, Central Office, and is the Administrative Officer for National Radiation Oncology Program.

In partnership with her family, Edwinette is the owner of Second Look Flea Mart, LLC. She and her husband are owners of Getting Up to Get Out: Financial Literacy Seminars, LLC. Edwinette is a charter member of the Top Ladies of Distinction, Inc., The Central Virginia Chapter and Literacy Chairman for this chapter.

She is married to her husband Paul and together they have one daughter and one granddaughter.

Eulica Kimber

Chapter 8: Get Your Mind Right

Eulica Kimber has been speaking and teaching the language of business, accounting, for over 25 years. As a Certified Public Accountant (CPA) and Master of Business Administration (MBA), her education and professional experience in accounting and entrepreneurship have given her the ability to help her clients by removing the fear and intimidation of the financial aspects of their businesses. She does this by creating customized action plans for the startup and growth of businesses through her online Plan2Pro$per Small Business Academy and one on one business coaching.

Visit: www.eulicakimbercpa.com

Lisa Williams

Chapter 9: Strength, Courage and Wisdom

Lisa F. Williams is the founder and Chief Consultant for Kingdom Consulting Group, LLC providing leadership training, event management and administrative services. Additionally, Lisa earned a B.S. in Interdisciplinary Studies (Business & Religion) and a M.A. in Executive Leadership from Liberty University. Lisa has served in Leadership Roles in corporate America for the last 30 years.

When Lisa is not running projects, she is passionate about grooming the next level leader; whether it is mentoring her staff, new entrepreneurs, ministry leaders or preparing young ladies for leadership roles in the community.

Visit: kingdomconsulting.biz | facebook.com/lisafrancinewilliams

Sharvette Mitchell

Chapter 10: Your Presence Matters

Sharvette Mitchell is a graduate of Virginia Commonwealth University with a Bachelor of Science in Marketing. She brings to the table, 25 years past experience in corporate America in the field of training & development, and Consumer Compliance.

Sharvette, often referred to as the Platform Builder, provides consulting services and web design/branding services for entrepreneurs so that they can generate more revenue with an amazing personal brand. In addition, Sharvette is a speaker & trainer who speaks and trains on online marketing strategies, Social Media marketing, personal branding, and creation of digital products & courses.

She is a Professional Certified Leadership Coach, Board member for James River Writers, a past recipient of the ACHI Magazine's – Radio Personality of The Year Award and has been featured in publications such as Huffington Post, HOPE for Women Magazine, CEO Magazine, Glambitious Magazine, Rescue A CEO Blog & Sista Sense Magazine. Sharvette has also been seen on CBS 6 Monday Motivation, CBS 6 Virginia This Morning, The CW Network, and Comcast Cable.

For over 12 years, she has hosted a weekly talk radio show, The Sharvette Mitchell Radio Show, that airs on Blog Talk Radio, iTunes, iHeart Radio, and on six LIVE STREAMING platforms.

Lastly, Sharvette is the visionary author of the anthologies, PROPEL - The Essential Handbook for Emerging Women in Business & Leadership and POUR - The Secret Effects of Giving and Serving in Small Business and Leadership.

Find more out at www.Mitchell-Productions.com

www.ingramcontent.com/pod-product-compliance
Lightning Source LLC
Chambersburg PA
CBHW071709210326
41597CB00017B/2403